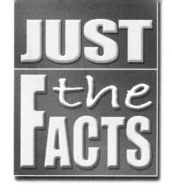

SOLAR SYSTEM

This edition published in the United States in 2006 by School Specialty Publishing, a member of the School Specialty Family.
Copyright © ticktock Entertainment Ltd 2006 First published in Great Britain in 2006 by ticktock Media Ltd. Printed in China.

Written by Steve Parker.

Library of Congress-in-Publication Data is on file with the publisher.

Send all inquiries to:
School Specialty Publishing
8720 Orion Place
Columbus, OH 43240-2111

ISBN 0-7696-4259-4
1 2 3 4 5 6 7 8 9 10 TTM 11 10 09 08 07 06

CONTENTS

HOW TO USE THIS BOOK

JUST THE FACTS, SOLAR SYSTEM is a quick and easy-to-use way to look up facts about our solar system. Every page is packed with cut-away diagrams, charts, scientific terms and key pieces of information. For fast access to just the facts, follow the tips on these pages.

BOX HEADINGS
Look for heading words linked to your research to guide you to the right fact box

INTRODUCTION TO TOPIC

TWO QUICK WAYS TO FIND A FACT:

1 Look at the detailed **CONTENTS** list on page 3 to find your topic of interest.

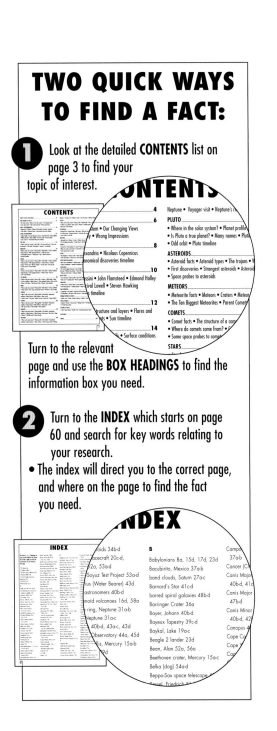

Turn to the relevant page and use the **BOX HEADINGS** to find the information box you need.

2 Turn to the **INDEX** which starts on page 60 and search for key words relating to your research.
• The index will direct you to the correct page, and where on the page to find the fact you need.

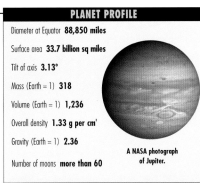

JUPITER

Jupiter is by far the biggest planet in the solar system. It is a vast plane of swirling gases and storms of unimaginable fury. As the fifth planet out, it is the nearest *gas giant*, a planet made almost completely of gases, to the Sun. It is not much smaller than some of the stars called *brown dwarfs*. Jupiter does not shine itself, but reflects sunlight as all planets do. Even so, its huge pull of gravity holds more than 60 moons in orbit around it Jupiter is named after the Roman king of the gods, also called *Jove*.

PLANET PROFILE

Diameter at Equator **88,850 miles**

Surface area **33.7 billion sq miles**

Tilt of axis **3.13°**

Mass (Earth = 1) **318**

Volume (Earth = 1) **1,236**

Overall density **1.33 g per cm³**

Gravity (Earth = 1) **2.36**

Number of moons **more than 60**

A NASA photograph of Jupiter.

MAJOR FEATURES

Jupiter has several distinctive features mapped by astronomers.

Great Red Spot
A giant storm system three times wider than Earth, that travels around Jupiter just south of the equator, once every 6 days.

White Spot
Smaller circulatory storm systems in Jupiter's atmosphere, about the size of Earth.

Browns Spots
Stormy regions that are probably warmer than surrounding clouds.

Rings
These consist of dust knocked fro Jupiter's moons by meteor strikes

Inner Structure
Central small rocky core, then a layer of "metallic" hydrogen, the liquid hydrogen, and finally the outermost atmosphere of mainly hydrogen gas. These layers flow from one to another, with no sha boundaries.

ATMOSPHERIC CONDITIONS

ATMOSPHERE:
Mostly hydrogen, some helium, traces of methane, water vapor, ammonia, hydrogen sulphide, and other gases

NATURE OF SURFACE:
Visible surface is whirling gases, possibly a solid surface on a small rocky core miles below visible surface

AVERAGE CLOUD-TOP SURFACE TEMP: -202°F

LOWEST CLOUD-TOP SURFACE TEMP: -261°F

HIGHEST CLOUD-TOP SURFACE TEMP: -277°F

WEATHER OR CLIMATE:
Complete cloud coverage with storms and wind speeds up to 272.84 mph.

SEASONAL CHANGES:
Few, being so far from Sun

A shot of Jupiter's atmosphere.

ORBIT DETAILS

Average distance from Sun
483.6 million miles

Average distance from Sun
5.203 AU (Earth = 1)

Closest distance to Sun (perihelion) 460.27 million miles

Farthest distance from Sun (aphelion) 507.12 million miles

Average orbital speed
8.07 miles per second

Slowest orbital speed
7.7 miles per second

Fastest orbital speed
8.5 miles per second

Time for one orbit
(Jupiter year) 11.87 Earth years

Axial rotation period
(Jupiter day) 9.92 Earth days

Sun

Jupiter

Jupiter's Giant Red Spot.

• See page 55 for information on probes to Jupiter.

SCIENTIFIC DIAGRAMS
Clear, accurate diagrams explain difficult astronomic concepts.

• See page 55 for information on probes to Jupiter.

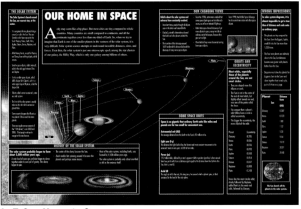
6–7 Our Home in Space

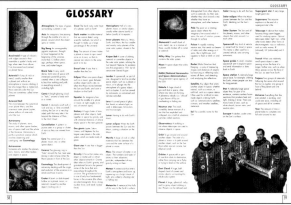
58–59 Glossary

OTHER FEATURES

- **BELTS** Strips of dark clouds that wind from west to east (left to right) and change through the years.

- **ZONES** Lengths of light-colored clouds that change like the darker belts. Blue-tinted clouds are the lowest and warmest. Zones contain higher clouds than belts.

- **TURBULENCE** Belts sometimes move in the opposite direction to their neighboring zones, creating swirling patterns of storms and turbulence along their edges.

MOON RECORDS

- Ganymede is the largest moon in the solar system.

- Callisto is the most heavily cratered object.

- Io probably has the most volcanic activity.

NASA images showing IO volcanoes produce red- and black-colored lava flows and yellow sulphur patches.

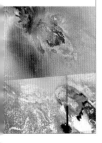

JUPITER'S RINGS

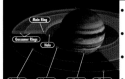

- **MAIN RING** Dust from Adrastea and Metis moons.
- **FIRST GOSSAMER RING** Dust from Thebe moon.
- **SECOND GOSSAMER RING** Dust from Amalthea moon.
- **FAINT OUTER RING**

Main Ring · Gossamer Rings · Halo · Amalthea · Adrastea · Metis · Thebe

TRUE GIANT

Jupiter has more than twice as much mass than all the other eight planets added together. However, it would probably need to be 50 times heavier to start burning like a true star.

SPEED SPIN

Jupiter is not only the largest planet, it also spins around the fastest, once in less than 10 Earth hours. The spinning speed of the upper atmosphere at the equator is 5 minutes faster than at the poles, so the atmosphere is continually being twisted and torn.

JUPITER'S MOONS

On January 7–11, 1610, Galileo discovered Jupiter's four main moons, now known as *Galilean moons*, by following their orbits across the face of the planet.

This was direct evidence that the Earth was not at the center of everything. It also strengthened his idea that planets like Earth and Jupiter probably revolved around the Sun.

MOON (or group)	DIAMETER	DISTANCE FROM JUPITER
Inner group	Four small moons less than 125 miles across	Less than 136,702 miles
Io	2,263 miles	124,280 miles
Europa	1,1939 miles	262,044 miles
Ganymede	3,270 miles	664,818 miles
Callisto	2,995 miles	1,169,475 miles
Themisto	4.97 miles	4,592,146 miles
Himalia group	Most under 62.14 miles	6.8–7.5 milllion miles
Ananke group	Most under 62.14 miles	13 million miles
Carme group	Most under 62.14 miles	14 million miles
Pasiphaë	Small outermost moons	14 million miles

JUPITER TIMELINE

3,000 years ago
Jupiter was known to Greeks and then the Romans.

1,500 years ago
In Ancient China, Jupiter was known as the *Wood Star.*

1610
Galileo observed Jupiter's four largest moons.

1665
The Great Red Spot was first observed.

1690
Giovanni Domenico Cassini noticed that the upper atmosphere takes longer to spin at the poles than around the equator.

1973
US *Pioneer 10* probe flew past.

1979
Voyager 1 flew past taking spectacular photographs. *Voyager 2* achieved similar results.

1992
Ulysses probe passes by Jupiter on its way to the Sun, taking measurements.

1994
Parts of comet *Shoemaker-Levy 9* hit Jupiter in July, photographed by the approaching *Galileo* space probe.

1995
Galileo became the first probe to orbit Jupiter on December 7. On the same day, an atmosphere probe it had already released parachuted 94 miles into the atmosphere, collecting information for almost one hour.

1996–2003
Galileo continued its studies of Jupiter and its nearer moons, flying past many of them several times.

2000
The Great Red Spot had shrunk to about half its size in 1900.

2000
Cassini probe passes on way to Saturn.

2003
Galileo plunged into the clouds in September.

2007
The *New Horizons* probe is due to fly past, on its way to Pluto.

2010
The US Jupiter probe *Juno* is scheduled for launch. *Juno* will orbit over Jupiter's poles.

25

TIMELINES

Important events are listed in chronological order.

For fast access to facts in the timelines, look for key words in the headings.

1992
Ulysses probe passes by Jupiter on its way to the Sun taking measurements.

GLOSSARY

- A GLOSSARY of words and terms used in this book begins on page 58.

- The glossary words provide additional information to supplement the facts on the main pages.

JUST THE FACTS

Each topic box presents the facts you need in short, easy-to-follow information.

LINKS

Look for the purple links throughout the book. Each link gives details of other pages where related or additional facts can be found.

The Solar System is based around the Sun, our nearest star, at the center.

- It is comprised of nine planets that go around, or orbit, the Sun. They are (listed in order from nearest to the Sun) Mercury, Venus, Earth, Mars, Jupiter, Saturn, Uranus, Neptune, and Pluto.

- All of these planets, except for Mercury and Venus, have orbiting objects, called *moons*.

- Smaller space objects, called *asteroids*, orbit in the wide gap between Mars and Jupiter.

- Similar smaller space objects, called *KBOs* (Kuiper Belt Objects), orbit in a wide region beyond Neptune, called the *Kuiper Belt*.

- Objects called *comets* occasionally enter our solar system.

- The limit of the solar system is usually taken as the orbit of the outermost planet Pluto.

- Some experts disagree that Pluto is a true planet. Others search for more planets.

- There are regular announcements of the "10th planet," as in 2003 and 2005. Most people continue to recognize the nine for now.

OUR HOME IN SPACE

A city may seem like a big place. But most cities are tiny compared to whole countries. Many countries are small compared to continents, and all the continents together cover less than one-third of Earth. So, when we try to imagine that Earth is one of the smaller planets in the vastness of the solar system, it is very difficult. Solar system science attempts to understand incredible distances, sizes, and forces. Even then, the solar system is just one microscopic speck among the star clusters of our galaxy, the Milky Way, which is only one galaxy among billions of others.

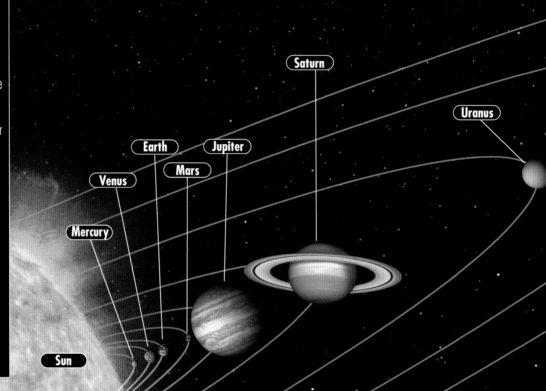

HISTORY OF THE SOLAR SYSTEM

The solar system probably began to form about 5,000 million years ago.

- A vast cloud of space gas and dust began to clump together under its own pull of gravity. The clump began to spin.

- The center of the clump became the Sun.

- Much smaller bits spinning around it became the planets and perhaps some moons.

- Most of the solar system, including Earth, was formed by 4,500 million years ago.

- The solar system is probably only about one-third as old as the universe itself.

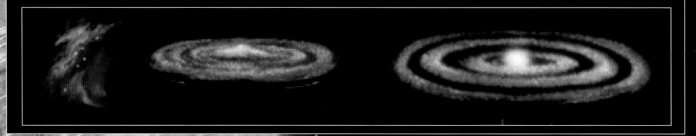

Beliefs about the solar system and universe have constantly evolved.

- In ancient times, people thought all objects seen in the skies went around Earth.

- Gradually, scientific observations showed that Earth and other planets orbited the Sun.

- The invention of the telescope around 1609 confirmed this idea and allowed the discovery of many more space objects.

- From the 1930s, astronomers realized that some space objects gave out invisible radio waves, as well as or instead of light rays.

- Radio telescopes allowed discovery of yet more objects in space, many invisible to ordinary optical telescopes, because they give out no light.

- More kinds of rays were discovered coming from space objects.

- From 1990, the Hubble Space Telescope has discovered more stars and other space objects.

In solar system diagrams, it is almost impossible to get a true idea of distance and scale onto an ordinary page.

- The planets are tiny compared to the Sun. Even the biggest, Jupiter, would fit into the Sun more than 1,000 times.

- The four inner planets are relatively close to the Sun, but distances become ever greater with planets farther from the Sun.

- Diagrams must show the planets far biggerm closer to the Sunm and closer together than in real scale, just to fit them on a page.

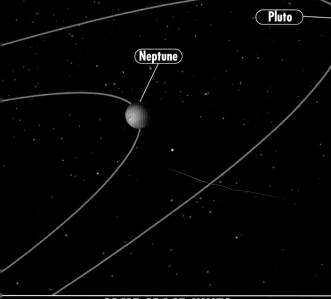

Pluto

Neptune

ORBITS AND ECCENTRICITY

Most orbits, especially those of the planets around the Sun, are not exact circles.

- They are shaped more like ellipses or ovals.

- The Sun is not in the center of the oval of most orbits, but slightly offset toward one end, near one of the points called the *focus*.

- The amount that a planet's orbit differs from a circle is called *eccentricity*.

- The bigger the eccentricity, the more elliptical the orbit.

Planet	Eccentricity
Mercury	0.205
Venus	0.006
Earth	0.016
Mars	0.093
Jupiter	0.048
Saturn	0.054
Uranus	0.047
Neptune	0.008
Pluto	0.248

Venus has the most circular orbit, closely followed by Neptune, while Pluto's is the most oval orbit, followed by Mercury.

SOME SPACE UNITS

Space is so gigantic that ordinary Earth units like miles and pounds are far too small for convenient use.

Astronomical unit (AU)
The average distance from the Earth to the Sun is 93 million miles.

Light year (l-y)
The distance that light (which has the fastest and most constant movement in the universe) travels in one year, is 5.88 trillion miles.

Parsec (pc)
19.2 trillion miles, defined by a star's apparent shift in position (parallax) when viewed from two points which are a distance apart equal to the distance from the Earth to the Sun, that is, one AU.

Axial tilt
The angle at which the axis, the imaginary line around which a planet spins, is tilted compared to the level of the solar plane.

Planet	Distance from Sun (AU)
Mercury	0.387
Venus	0.723
Earth	1.00
Mars	1.52
Jupiter	5.20
Saturn	9.54
Uranus	19.19
Neptune	30.01
Pluto	39.48

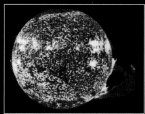

The Sun dwarfs all the planets in the solar system.

27,000 years ago
First stone age rock carvings of the Sun and Moon.

5,000 years ago
Egyptians introduce a year with 365 days, which proceeded our modern calendar.

4,500 years ago
Mars known by the Egyptians as the *Red One*.

4,300 years ago
Chinese make first record of solar eclipse.

4,000 years ago
Babylonian priests made some of the first records of astronomical observations.

3,500 years ago
Venus known to Babylonians.

2,455 years ago
Anaxagoras of Ancient Greece suggested the Sun was made of hot rocks.

2,360 years ago
Chinese astronomers may have spotted the moons of Jupiter.

2,265 years ago
Aristarchus proposed the Sun was the center of the solar system.

2,000 years ago
Jupiter and Saturn known to Greeks and Romans.

1,855 years ago
Ptolemy's view of the solar system, based on Aristotle's belief that the Earth was the center of the solar system, begins to dominate beliefs for 1,400 years.

1543
Copernicus revived the suggestion of Aristarcus.

1608
Lippershey invented the optical telescope.

1609
Galileo began his space studies.

1609
Kepler published his first laws of planetary motion.

EARLY ASTRONOMERS

The earliest astronomers were not interested in how the universe worked, but when to plant or harvest crops and when rivers would flood. They used the movements of objects in the skies to make calendars, and to predict events in the future. Consequently, they became astrologers as well as astronomers. It was the ancient Greeks who first started to ask questions about the universe and how it worked. Their work was followed by the studies of great European astronomers from the 15th century onward.

HIPPARCHUS OF RHODES

Lifetime: Between 190–120 BC

Nationality: Greek

Major Achievements:

- Hipparchus was believed to have cataloged over 800 stars. He also studied the motions of the Moon.

- He invented a brightness scale, subsequently developed by later generations of astronomers into a scale referred to as *magnitude*.

- Hipparchus calculated the length of the Earth's year to within 6 1/2 minutes.

An illustration of the early astonomer Hipparchus.

• See page 40 MAGNITUDE

PTOLEMY OF ALEXANDRIA

Lifetime: AD 87–150

Nationality: Greek

Major Achievements:

- Ptolemy wrote many books containing Greek ideas and observations collected over the past 500 years, including *Almagest*, also called *the Greatest*.

- Ptolemy described more than 1,000 stars in his books, including 48 different constellations.

- The astronomer also made early calculations of the size and distance of the Sun and Moon.

- Ptolemy devised a geocentric system with Earth at the center of the universe. His order for closest to farthest from Earth was the Moon, Mercury, Venus, Sun, Mars, Jupiter, and Saturn.

The Greek astronomer Ptolemy.

NICOLAUS COPERNICUS

Lifetime: 1473–1543

Nationality: Polish

Major Achievements:

- Copernicus realized the geocentric system dating back to Ptolemy was inaccuarate.

- He devised a new heliocentric, meaning *Sun-centered system*. Copernicus stated that the Earth and all the other planets revolved around a stationary, central Sun.

- Copernicus' ideas were incorporated in his book *The Revolution of the Heavenly Spheres*, completed in 1530.

- The book was not published until 1543, perhaps just a few days before he died.

The Polish astronomer Nicolaus Copernicus.

TYCHO BRAHE

A bronze statue of Tycho Brahe in Prague.

Lifetime: 1546–1601

Nationality: Danish

Major Achievements:

- Brahe discovered a supernova in Cassiopeia in 1572, now called *Tycho's Star*. He suggested this was a star outside the solar system that did not move.

- Brahe plotted the accurate positions of 780 stars over 20 years.

- The astronomer employed Johannes Kepler as his assistant to help him with his studies.

- Kepler completed and published Brahe's star catalogue, *Rudolphine Tables*, in 1627.

TABULÆ

RUDOLPHINÆ.

QUIBVS ASTRONOMICÆ SCIENTIÆ, TEMPO-

TYCHONE

IOANNES KEPLERUS.

The title page and an illustration from Brahe's *Rudolphine Tables*, completed by Kepler.

JOHANNES KEPLER

Lifetime: 1571–1630

Nationality: German

Major Achievements:

- Kepler joined Brahe in Prague in 1600 as his assistant.

- He devised the laws of planetary motion, linking a planet's orbit and speed to the Sun.

- The astronomer wrote the first astronomy textbook, *Epitome Astronomiae Copernicanae* (*Epitome of Copernican Astronomy*).

The German astronomer Johannes Kepler.

LATER ASTRONOMERS

After the telescope was invented, many more people began looking at the night sky. Some had little science background, and did it as a hobby, but chanced upon an amazing discovery that put their name forever into history. Others were full-time professional astronomers who spent a lifetime observing and recording, yet their names are known to very few. Even now, millions of people watch the skies every night.

Astronomy
General study of objects in space including the stars, planets, moons, and galaxies. Often includes observing and recording.

Astrophysics
The physical nature of stars, planets, and other space bodies, including their make-up and contents, temperatures and pressures, and densities and conditions.

Cosmology
Study of the origins, history, make-up, and fate of the universe as a whole. Often carried out using mathematics and physics, rather than stargazing.

Space science
Often more concerned with spacecraft, probes, rockets and other hardware, and the conditions for space travellers.

GALILEO GALILEI

Lifetime: 1564–1642

Nationality: Italian

Major Achievements:

- Galileo improved the first telescopes and was the first person to use them for scientific studies of the night sky.

- He observed mountains and craters on the Moon, many stars too faint to see with the unaided eye, and four of Jupiter's moons.

- Galileo recorded his early discoveries in his book *Sidereal Messenger* (1610).

- Galileo believed in Copernicus' ideas that the Sun, not the Earth, was the center of the solar system, as had been previously stated by Ptolemy.

- He put forward both sets of theories in his book *Dialogue on Two Chief World Systems* (1632). This work was heavily criticized and the astronomer was put under house arrest by religious leaders for his views.

- Galileo made advances in many other areas of science including the mechanics of moving objects, like swinging pendulums, falling canonballs, and bullets.

• See page 8 for information on PTOLEMY.

GIOVANNI DOMENICO CASSINI

Lifetime: 1625–1712

Nationality: Italian-French

Major Achievements:

- Cassini was appointed as Director of the Paris Observatory in 1669.

- He made many discoveries, including four satellites of Saturn and the gap in Saturn's rings, now named the *Cassini Division*.

- Cassini made many advances combining his observations with calculations, including the orbit times of Mars, Venus, and Jupiter, the paths of Jupiter's moons, and the first fairly accurate distance between the Earth and the Sun (the AU, Astronomical Unit).

JOHN FLAMSTEED

Lifetime: 1646–1719

Nationality: British

Major Achievements:

- Flamsteed became the first Astronomer Royal in 1675.

- He made the first extensive star charts using the telescope as part of work aimed at giving sailors a better method of navigation. The charts recorded the positions of over 2,935 stars.

- Due to a dispute with Isaac Newton and the Royal Society, the charts were published six years after he died.

EDMOND HALLEY

Lifetime: 1656–1742

Nationality: British.

Major Achievements:

- Edmond Halley traveled to St. Helena in the South Atlantic at the age of 20 to make the first telescopic chart of stars as seen in the Southern Hemisphere.

- Halley became interested in comets after the "Great Comet" of 1680. He worked out from historical records that a comet seen in 1531, 1607, and 1682 should return in 1758, which it did (now called *Halley's Comet*).

- The astronomer was the first to suggest that nebulae were clouds of dust and gas where stars might form.

- Halley became Astronomer Royal in 1720 and began an 18-year study of the complete revolution of the moon.

- Halley's other activities included studying archaeology, geophysics, and the history of astronomy.

WILLIAM HERSCHEL

Lifetime: 1738–1822

Nationality: German-British

Major Achievements:

- Herschel made many of his own telescopes.

- He discovered the planet Uranus in 1781 and some moons of Uranus and Saturn.

- During his lifetime, Herschel cataloged over 800 double-stars.

- He also published a chart of over 5,000 nebulae in 1820.

- Herschel also recognized that the Milky Way was a flattened disc of stars.

EDWIN HUBBLE

Lifetime: 1889–1953

Nationality: American

Major Achievements:

- Working mostly at Mount Wilson Observatory, Hubble's studies of nebulae, such as parts of Andromeda, showed they were masses of stars.

- Hubble concluded that these star masses were galaxies outside our own Milky Way.

- He introduced a system of classifying galaxies by their shapes.

- Hubble measured the speed of galaxies in 1929 and showed farther ones move faster, leading to Hubble's Law and the idea that the universe is expanding.

PERCIVAL LOWELL

Lifetime: 1855–1916

Nationality: American

Major Achievements:

- Lowell became interested in astronomy after reports by Schiaparelli of channels on Mars. *Channels* was misunderstood as *canals,* and Lowell became convinced of the existence of Martians, even writing books on them.

- He established the Lowell Observatory in Arizona in 1894, mainly to study Mars.

- Lowell predicted the existence of another planet beyond Neptune (eventually discovered Pluto in 1930 at Lowell's observatory).

STEPHEN HAWKING

Lifetime: 1940–

Nationality: British

Major Achievements:

- Hawking continued Einstein's ideas on time being a fourth dimension, and worked on the origin of the universe at the Big Bang.

- He worked on a common theory for the four basic forces in the universe, being gravity, electromagnetic, and strong and weak nuclear forces.

- Hawking made great advances to our understanding of black holes.

ASTRONOMICAL DISCOVERIES TIMELINE

1931
First radio telescope built.

1948
200-inch Hale reflector telescope first operated at Mount Palomar, California.

1962
First X-rays detected from space.

1963
First quasar (quasi-stellar object) discovered.

1967
First pulsar (spinning neutron star) discovered.

1976
240-inch reflector telescope first operated at Mount Semirodniki, USSR.

1986
Halley's comet returned.

1987
SN1987A became the first supernova to be seen with the unaided eye in modern times.

1990
Hubble Space Telescope sent into Earth orbit by the space shuttle *Discovery*.

1991
The probe *Galileo* approached within 16,000 miles of the asteroid *Gaspra*.

1992
COBE satellite detected microwave "echoes" of the Big Bang.

2001
Genesis returned samples of the solar wind.

2004
Hubble Utra Deep Field revealed first galaxies to emerge from the "dark ages" less than 1,000 million years after the Big Bang.

2005
Deep Impact probe sent impactor device into comet *Tempel*.

2005
Astronomers announced the discovery of *2003UB313*, the largest object to be found in the solar system since Pluto.

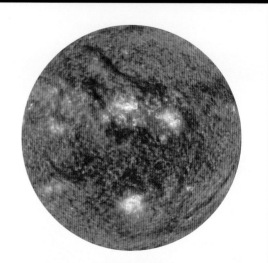

THE SUN

Our closest star, the Sun, is the center of the solar system. All the planets and asteroids are held in their orbits by its immense gravity. It also attracts objects from the farthest reaches of the solar system, such as comets. For billions of years, the Sun has been providing Earth with light that green plants use as an energy source for living and growing. Herbivorous animals eat the plants, and carnivorous animals eat the herbivores. In this way, the Sun powers life on Earth.

ORBIT DETAILS

Average distance from center of Milky Way 26,000 light years

Time for one orbit around center 225 million years

Average orbital speed 135 miles per second

Time for one revolution 25.38 days at equator

STAR PROFILE

Diameter at Equator	**864,938 miles (109 time Earth's)**
Surface area	**109^{109} sq miles (12,000 times Earth)**
Mass	**2×10^{27} tons (333,000 times Earth)**
Volume	**33×10^{16} cubic miles (1.3 million times Earth)**
Overall density	**99 lbs. per square foot**
Gravity (Earth = 1)	**27.9**
Number of main planets	**9 (debated)**

A NASA photograph of the Sun.

STRUCTURE AND LAYERS

CORE
- About 174,000 miles across.
- Nuclear fusion reactions convert hydrogen to helium, producing immense amounts of light, heat, and other radiation.
- Energy output equivalent to Earth's largest power plants do in a year, every second.

RADIATIVE ZONE
- About 220,000 miles deep.
- Conveys heat and light outwards by photon transfer between ions.
- Temperature falls with distance from the core.

CONVECTIVE ZONE
- About 125,000 miles deep.
- Super-hot material carries heat outwards from radiative zone.
- Material cools at photosphere and sinks back to receive more heat.
- The result is in-and-out convection currents.

PHOTOSPHERE
- Visible surface of the Sun.
- Varies in depth from 621 miles.
- Emits photons of light and other energy forms into space.

CHROMOSPHERE
- About 6,221 miles deep.
- Visible as a red-colored flash around the Sun at the start and end of a total solar eclipse.

CORONA
- Wispy outer atmosphere around the Sun.
- Extends many millions of miles into space, to distances bigger than the Sun itself.

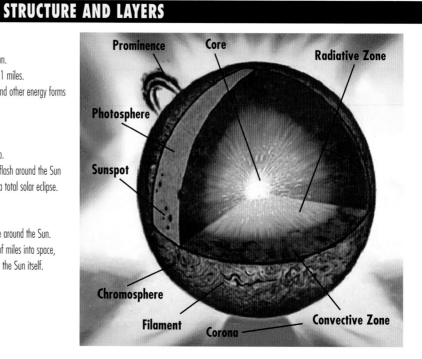

FLARES AND PROMINENCES

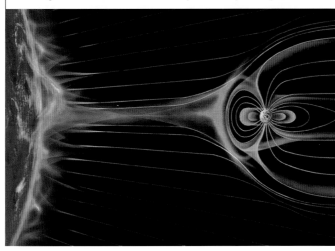

- Solar flares are massive explosions in the lower corona and chromosphere.

- They were first observed by Richard Carrington in 1859.

- Trigger massive solar eruptions *called coronal mass ejections.*

- Solar prominences are larger and longer-lasting than flares.

- Many leap up, along, and down in a curved arc back to the Sun.

- Typically, prominences are thousands of miles long.

- Largest ones are 310,000 or more miles long.

MAKE-UP OF PHOTOSPHERE

0.7 0.3 0.7%

24.8

73.5%

Key

- Carbon
- Oxygen
- Helium
- Hydrogen
- Traces

SOLAR WIND

- Solar wind steams away from the Sun in all directions.

- It reaches speeds of up to 250 miles per second and comes mainly from the corona.

- Solar wind consists of charged particles, ions, and other particles in a form called *plasma.*

- Where it interacts with Earth's magnetic fields, near the North and South Poles, it creates an aurora, shimmering light high in the sky, calle the *Northern Lights* (Aurora Borealis) and *Southern Lights* (Aurora Australis).

• See pages 11 and 54
SOLAR WIND

A diagram of solar wind. The Earth is protected by its magnetic field.

SUNSPOTS

Sunspots are cooler variable patches on the photosphere, probably caused by magnetic interactions.

- The inner umbra of each spot is around 7,232°F. The outer penumbra is about 9,932°F.

- They were first noticed to vary in a regular way by Heinrich Schwabe between 1826 and 1843.

- Sunspots usually vary in an 11-year cycle. An average sunspot "life" is 2 weeks.

- On March 30, 2001, *SOHO* (Solar and Heliospheric Observatory) recorded the largest sunspot group so far, covering more than 13 times the area of the Earth.

NASA photo of a sunspot.

Close-up of a sunspot.

TEMPERATURES

Corona 35.6 million °F   **Surface** 10,000 °F   **Core** 27 million °F

SUN TIMELINE

27,000 years ago
Depicted in rock carvings in Europe, North Africa, and Australia.

From 7,000 years ago
Sun worshipped as a god by many ancient civilizations.

4,900 years ago
First phase of construction of Stonehenge, a Sun-aligned stone-age temple in England.

From 4,000 years ago
The Sun worshipped as Ra in ancient Egypt.

2,030 years ago
Chinese astronomers first mentioned sunspots.

AD 1300s
Aztec people made sacrifices to their Sun god, *Huitzilopochtli.*

1610
Sunspots first seen through a telescope by Johannes and David Fabricius, then by Galileo.

1962
McMath Pierce Solar Telescope in Arizona is largest telescope dedicated to Sun study.

1990
Ulysses probe launched from a space shuttle to study the Sun's North and South Poles. It also studied solar wind.

1995
Joint European/US probe *SOHO* was launched on December 2.

1997
ACE (Advanced Composition Explorer) satellite launched to study particles and materials from the Sun and elsewhere.

2001
Space probe *Genesis* was launched on August 8 to capture samples of the solar wind.

2004
On September 8, *Genesis* returned but was damaged on crash-landing.

2005
Preliminary results announced from *Genesis.*

MERCURY

Known by most ancient people by its brief periods of visibility at dawn and dusk, Mercury was named after the Roman winged messenger of the gods. It has the fastest orbital speed of any planet, averaging 30 miles every second. Being the closest planet to the Sun, it is blasted by solar heat and other radiation. This has an extremely weak atmosphere. Mercury's daytime side heats to incredible temperatures, however, the night side plunges to within -275°F.

PLANET PROFILE

Diameter at Equator **3032 miles**

Surface area **75 million sq km**

Tilt of axis **0.01°**

Mass (Earth = 1) **0.055**

Volume (Earth = 1) **0.056**

Overall density **5.42 g per cm³**

Gravity (Earth = 1) **0.377**

Number of moons **0**

A NASA photograph of the planet Mercury.

MAJOR FEATURES

Less than half of Mercury's surface has been mapped in any detail, so its surface features are less known than most other planets.

Caloris Basin
Massive crater made by asteroid/meteoroid impact, measuring 800 miles across.

Caloris Montes
Curved ranges with peaks rising to 9800 feet sited at one of the hottest places on Mercury, within the Caloris Basin crater.

Discovery Scarp
Joining two craters, this cliff is 217 miles long and its maximum height is around 9,200 feet.

SURFACE CONDITIONS

ATMOSPHERE:
Almost zero, traces of potassium, argon, oxygen, and argon

NATURE OF SURFACE:
Bare iron-rich rocks pitted with hundreds of large craters

AVERAGE SURFACE TEMPERATURE: 338°F

LOWEST SURFACE TEMPERATURE: -275°F

HIGHEST SURFACE TEMPERATURE: 840°F

WEATHER OR CLIMATE:
None due to lack of atmosphere

SEASONAL CHANGES:
None due to almost zero tilt of axis

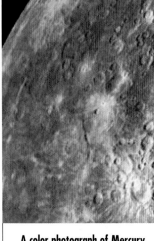

A color photograph of Mercury showing the pitted iron-rich surface.

ORBIT DETAILS

Average distance from Sun
35,980,000 miles

Average distance from Sun
0.387 AU (Earth =1)

Closest distance to Sun (perihelion) 28,580,000 miles

Farthest distance from Sun (aphelion) 69.8 million km

Average orbital speed
29.5 miles per second

Slowest orbital speed
24.1 miles per second

Fastest orbital speed
36.6 miles per second

Time for one orbit
(Mercury year) 87.9 Earth days

Axial rotation period
(Mercury day) 176 Earth days

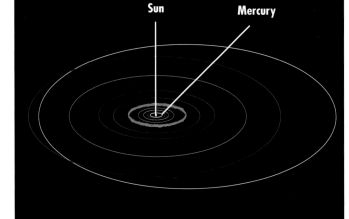

Sun   Mercury

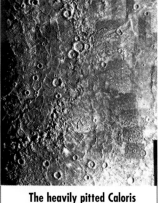

The heavily pitted Caloris Basin crater.

• See pages 34–37 for information on ASTEROIDS and METEORS.

OTHER GEOLOGICAL FEATURES

- **SCARPS (RUPES)** Long cliff-like ridges with one steep side and one gradually sloping side.

- **RIDGES (DORSA)** Long, prominent ridges with two steep sides, formed as Mercury's core cooled, shrank, and the already solid crust cracked into wrinkles.

- **YOUNGER PLAINS** Uplands probably formed from hardened lava flows, less marked by craters from impacts.

- **OLDER PLAINS** Lowlands much more pockmarked with overlapping craters than the younger plains.

- **ARECIBO VALLIS** Valley named after the Arecibo Observatory, home of Earth's largest radio telescope, in Puerto Rico.

- **ICE** Despite Mercury's incredible heat, there is probably ice at its North Pole, in deep craters with permanent shade from the Sun.

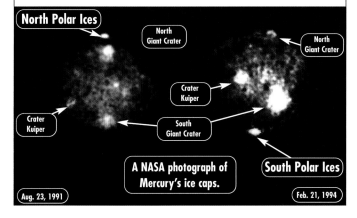

North Polar Ices
North Giant Crater
North Giant Crater
Crater Kuiper
Crater Kuiper
South Giant Crater
South Polar Ices
A NASA photograph of Mercury's ice caps.
Aug. 23, 1991
Feb. 21, 1994

SMALL AND CURIOUS

The size of Mercury is shown in the above picture of the planet (circled in red) travelling past the sun.

- Mercury is the second-smallest planet in the Solar System, after Pluto.

- It has a very oval-shaped orbit, much more than most other planets. Only outermost Pluto is more eccentric.

- Its axis is hardly tilted at all, so the Sun is always directly over its equator all through its year.

MERCURY TIMELINE

5,000 years ago
The Sumerians mentioned Mercury, whom they call *Ubu-idim-gud-ud.*

3,300 years ago
Earliest detailed observations of Mercury in ancient Babylon.

2,500 years ago
In ancient Greece, Mercury (like Venus) was thought to be two different planets with two names— *Apollo* in the dawn sky and *Hermes* at dusk.

2,470 years ago
Heraclitus thought that Mercury, along with Venus, orbited the Sun rather than the Earth.

1,000 years ago
Ancient Chinese documents refer to Mercury as the *Water Star.*

1639
Giovanni Zupi's telescope observations showed different parts of Mercury were lit at different times by the Sun.

1965
Radar measurements showed that Mercury does not spin once but three times for every two orbits.

1973
US *Mariner 10* launched November 3 to fly past Venus and Mercury.

1974
Mariner 10 made its first flybys of Venus in February of Venus, and in March of Mercury, mapping about two-fifths of each planet's surface.

1974
Mariner 10 makes second flyby.

1975
Mariner 10's third flyby in March sends information on magnetic fields.

1961–62
The *Mercury* program of single-seat craft was the first to carry US astronauts into space.

2004
US *Mercury* probe *Messenger* launched in August.

2008–09
Messenger due to make three flybys of Mercury.

2011
Messenger due to enter Mercury orbit in March and survive for a year to study the thin atmosphere.

DISTINGUISHING FEATURES

Mercury has several features that distinguish from other planets.

Mercury has several hundred named craters, with names like *Shakespeare, Mark Twain, Dickens, Beethoven, Chopin, Degas,* and *Sibelius.* All of its craters are named after famous artists and classical musicians.

In 1974, the *Mariner 10* spacecraft produced this image of the 27 mile wide Degas crater.

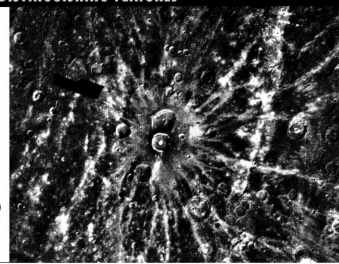

TEMPERATURE

Mercury has the widest temperature range of any planet, spanning almost 1112°F between day on the sunny side and night on the shady side. Earth's maximum range is less than 300°F.

SPINNING MERCURY

Because of its closeness to the Sun and slow spinning speed, at certain places and times on Mercury the Sun will rise just over the horizon, then go back and set, and then rise again—all on the same Mercury day.

MERCURY TRANSIT

Since Mercury is closer to the Sun than Earth, when the two planets are almost in line, Mercury appears to cross the Sun when viewed from Earth. This is called the *transit of Mercury.*

VENUS

Venus, the second planet from the Sun, is named after the Roman goddess of love and is shrouded in mystery. It is covered by thick swirling clouds of poisonous gases and droplets of acid that hide its surface from the view of outsiders. Although Venus is about the same size and mass as Earth, it could not be more different. It is the hottest of all the planets, partly because its thick atmosphere traps in vast amounts of heat from the nearby Sun in a greenhouse effect far more extreme than on Earth.

SURFACE CONDITIONS

ATMOSPHERE:
Thick, dense, mainly carbon dioxide, also nitrogen, and sulphur acids

NATURE OF SURFACE:
Hard and rocky, numerous volcanoes

AVERAGE SURFACE TEMPERATURE: 878°F

LOWEST SURFACE TEMPERATURE:
113°F (at cloud tops)

HIGHEST SURFACE TEMPERATURE:
932°F in valleys near the equator

WEATHER OR CLIMATE:
Thick swirling deadly-poisonous atmosphere, winds are 186 mph near its top

SEASONAL CHANGES:
Minimal on surface due to dense atmosphere

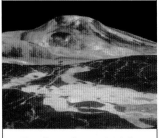

Magellan radar image of the volcano Sif Mons on Venus.

PLANET PROFILE

Diameter at Equator **7,520 miles**

Surface area **460 million sq km**

Tilt of axis **177.36°**

Mass (Earth = 1) **0.815**

Volume (Earth = 1) **0.856**

Overall density **5.2 g per cm³**

Gravity (Earth = 1) **0.90**

Number of moons **0**

A NASA mosaic of
the planet Venus.

ORBIT DETAILS

Average distance from Sun
67,240,000 miles

Average distance from Sun
0.723 AU (Earth =1)

**Closest distance to Sun
(perihelion)** 66,780,000 miles

**Farthest distance from Sun
(aphelion)** 67,690,000 miles

Average orbital speed
21.7 miles per second

Slowest orbital speed
21.6 miles per second

Fastest orbital speed
21.9 miles per second

Time for one orbit
(Venus year) 224.7 Earth days

Axial rotation period
(Venus day) 117 Earth days

Sun

Venus

MAJOR FEATURES

Several probes have been sent to Venus, and radio waves have been used to map virtually the entire planet.

Ishtar Terra
Northern highlands about the size of Australia, bearing Venus's highest mountains.

Maxwell Montes
Maxwell Mountains, a range about 540 miles long, with the highest peaks over 7 miles tall.

Lakshmi Planum
Vast upland plain partly encircled by Maxwell Mountains.

Aphrodite Terra
Southern uplands, roughly the size of South America.

Arachnoid Volcanoes
Photographed by the space probe *Magellan*, these have unusual ridges around them. The central volcano with its surrounding ridges looks like a giant spider.

A NASA photograph of the sprawling
Aphrodite Terra, shown in brown.

OTHER GEOLOGICAL FEATURES

- **CORONAE** Circular centers surrounded by ring-like ridges, the largest being Artemis Corona at 1,300 miles across.

- **PLAINS** Flat and fairly smooth, these cover two-thirds of the surface with low volcanoes up to 124 miles across.

- **MOUNTAINS** Six main mountain ranges cover about one-third of the surface.

- **UPLAND REGION** One of the largest is Beta Regio, about 3,280 feet deep.

- **LOWLAND DEPRESSIONS** Wide and low, include Atalanta Planitia, Guinevere Planitia, and Lavinia Planitia.

- **ALL FEATURES** All of Venus's surface features are named after females, either real people or from myth and legend, except Maxwell Mountains, named after scientist James Clerk Maxwell.

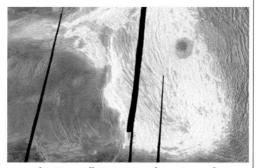

The Maxwell Mountains shot using radar.

TRANSIT OF VENUS

Since Venus is closer to the Sun than Earth, when the two planets are almost in line, Venus appears to cross the disc of the Sun when viewed from Earth. This is called the *transit of Venus*. The date it occurs and the time that Venus takes to cross the Sun's face have been used to estimate the distance between Earth and the Sun. Transits occur in pairs. The two in each pair are about eight years apart, but the time between pairs is more than 100 years.

The transit of Venus across the Sun.

• See page 18 for information on the Earth's orbit.

DAYTIME VIEWING

- Because of its closeness and bright reflection of sunlight, Venus is so bright that it is one of only two space bodies, other than the Sun, which can be seen during daylight from Earth. The other body is the Moon.

- It is also often the first star-like body to appear at dusk and the last to fade at dawn, earning it the names *Evening Star* and *Morning Star*.

REVERSE SPIN

Venus is one of only three planets with retrograde spin (the others are Uranus and Pluto). This means it spins on its axis in the opposite direction than the other planets. Seen from the side, its surface moves from east to west or right to left, or clockwise if viewed from above its North Pole.

NEAREST NEIGHBOR

No other planet comes closer to the Earth than Venus. At its closest, it is 23.7 million miles away.

ONE LONG DAY

Venus takes longer to spin once on its axis than to complete one orbit of the Sun.

CIRCULAR ORBIT

Most planets have an orbit that is an ellipse. The journey of Venus around the Sun is the most circular of all planets, meaning it has the least eccentric orbit of all the planets (especially compared to Mercury's).

UNDER PRESSURE

The atmosphere's pressing force or pressure on Venus (pictured below next to the Earth) is incredible — 90 times more than our own, and equivalent to the pressure almost 3,280 feet under the sea on Earth.

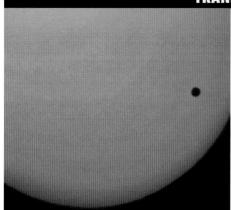

VENUS TIMELINE

3,600 years ago
Astronomical records in Babylonia record appearances of Venus.

3,500 years ago
Ancient Babylonians record Venus as one of the brightest "stars."

2,500 years ago
In ancient Greece, Venus was though to be two different planets with two names— *Phosphorus* in the dawn sky and *Hesperus* at dusk.

2,000 years ago
Ancient Chinese observers refer to Venus as the *Metal Star*.

1610
Galileo observed phases of Venus.

1639
First transit of Venus was observed.

1672
Giovanni Domenico Cassini claimed to discover moon of Venus.

1961
Russian space probe *Venera 1* aimed at Venus, but failed.

1962
US probe *Mariner 2* flew past Venus.

1966
Venera 3 probe crash-landed on the surface. *Venera 4* was more successful next year and sent back information. *Veneras 5, 6,* and *7* also sent back information.

1970
Venera 7 made the first successful landing.

1975
Venera 9 was the first probe to send a picture back from the surface of Venus, on October 21.

1978
US sent two *Pioneer* probes.

1990
The *Magellan* probe mapped all but 1/50 of the surface.

1998–99
Cassini-Huygens flew past Venus.

2004
First of a pair of transits witnessed.

2006
European Space Agency's *Venus Express* orbiter probe is due to arrive.

2012
Next transit of Venus due.

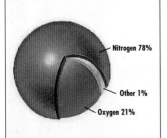

EARTH

Human beings may think of Earth as an "average" planet, but the more we learn about the rest of the solar system, the more we see that Earth is very unusual. This is mainly because its average surface temperature is just above 71°F. Earth has the smallest range of surface temperatures of any planet. Also, more than three-quarters of Earth's surface is rivers, lakes, seas, oceans, and frozen water as glaciers and ice-caps.

SURFACE CONDITIONS

ATMOSPHERE:
Almost four-fifths nitrogen, one-fifth oxygen, traces of carbon dioxide, water vapor, and other gases

NATURE OF SURFACE:
Varied from high rocky mountains to deep valleys and trenches, mostly covered with water

AVERAGE SURFACE TEMPERATURE: 71.6°F

LOWEST SURFACE TEMPERATURE: -130°F

HIGHEST SURFACE TEMPERATURE: 140°F

WEATHER OR CLIMATE:
Varies due to movement of atmosphere and its water vapor distributed by clouds and falling as rain, generally conditions become colder from the equator to the poles

SEASONAL CHANGES:
Marked seasons due to considerable tilt of axis, from cold winters and hot summers.

Nitrogen 78%

Other 1%

Oxygen 21%

PLANET PROFILE

Diameter at Equator **7,926 miles**

Surface area **196.9 million sq miles**

Tilt of axis **23.4°**

Mass **6.6 sextillion tons**

Volume **259.8 billion miles^3**

Overall density **5.517 g per cm^3**

Gravity **1g (9.8 miles per second^2)**

Number of moons **1**

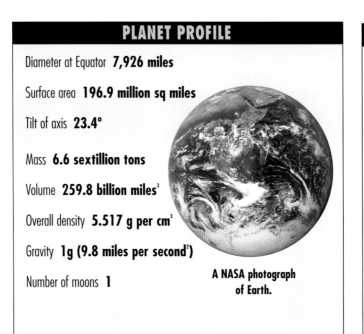

A NASA photograph of Earth.

ORBIT DETAILS

Average distance from Sun
92.9 million miles

Average distance from Sun
1.0 AU

Closest distance to Sun (perihelion) 91.4 million miles

Farthest distance from Sun (aphelion) 94.5 million miles

Average orbital speed
18.5 miles per second

Slowest orbital speed
18.2 miles per second

Fastest orbital speed
18.8 miles per second

Time for one orbit
(Earth year) 365.256 Earth days

Axial rotation period
(Earth day) 23.93 Earth hours

Sun

Earth

MAJOR FEATURES

Earth has been mapped extensively.

Rivers
The Amazon River of South America carries more water than the next five biggest rivers combined, emptying 6,350,000 cubic feet per second into the Atlantic Ocean.

Oceans
The Pacific Ocean covers almost half (46%) of the Earth's surface.

Mountains
The Himalayas of central Asia and northern India have eight of the world's ten tallest peaks.

Deserts
The Sahara Desert of North Africa is by far the greatest arid (very dry) area, covering more than 3.5 million square miles.

Lowest Point
The bottom of the deep-sea Challenger Deep in the north-west Pacific Ocean is 35,840 feet below the ocean's surface.

Highest Point
The peak of Mount Everest in the Himalayas is 29,035 feet above sea level.

Earth's highest mountain, Everest.

OTHER GEOLOGICAL FEATURES

The outer reef of the Great Barrier Reef.

- **LAKE SUPERIOR** is the largest body of fresh water by area.

- **LAKE BAIKAL** is the largest body of fresh water by volume.

- **THE LAMBERT GLACIER** on Antarctica is the largest glacier, at 311 miles long and 50 miles wide.

- **THE GRAND CANYON,** the most spectacular deep valley, has been worn away by the Colorado River. It is 277 miles long, up to 18 miles wide, and in places, 1 mile deep between almost sheer cliffs.

- **THE GREAT BARRIER REEF** is a long series of rocky reefs built over thousands of years by billions of tiny animals called coral *polyps*.

PLATE TECTONICS

- Researchers believe that the Earth's outer surface of thin rocky crust, is split into 12–15 giant curved pieces called *lithospheric plates*.

- Over millions of years, these slidearound the globe, at the rate of about 1-3 cm per year, carrying the major land masses with them in a process called *continental drift*.

- At the edges of some plates new rock is added by a process called *seafloor spreading*.

- Where two plates ram into each other, the crust buckles into mountains, such as the Himalayas and Andes.

- Where one plate slides below the other there are earthquakes and volcanoes.

POLAR ICE

- Apart from large cloud systems, the glistening ice caps over the North and South Poles are perhaps Earth's most noticeable feature from space.

- Each shrinks in summer, then spreads in winter, due to Earth's seasonal changes and zoned climate from the equator to the poles.

- The Arctic ice cap over the North Pole is a piece of ice up to 33 feet thick floating in the Arctic Ocean, with a winter extent of 9.3 million sq miles.

- The Antarctic ice cap over the South Pole covers the vast southern land mass of Antarctica, with a winter extent of 11.8 million sq miles.

LIFE

- Earth is the only planet in the solar system known to support life. This life depends on liquid water, which occurs in the narrow temperature range of 32 to 104°F.

- The greatest variety of land life occurs in tropical rainforests, which have 9 out of 10 of the more than 20 million species of plants, animals, and other life-forms.

- The richest variety of marine life is found in coral reefs.

- Many areas of wildlife are being affected, polluted, and used for agriculture and industry by the dominant life-form on Earth, human beings.

EARTH TIMELINE

Prehistory
More than 10,000 years ago, people made maps of their areas carved on stone or ivory, scratched into tablets, or woven into hangings.

3,000 years ago
Early Greeks believed the Earth was a flat disc.

2,500 years ago
In Ancient Greece, the idea grew that the world was round, based on observations such as how the stars vary at different places on Earth.

1519–1522
Ferdinand Magellan's expedition circled the globe to show that Earth was a sphere.

1785
James Hutton proposed his *Principle of Uniformitarianism*, which means the Earth's surface has been shaped over huge lengths of time by the same processes we see at work today—volcanoes, earthquakes, mountain-building, and erosion by wind, rain, ice, and snow. He believed the Earth was "immeasurably ancient."

1862
William Thomson calculated the Earth's age from its cooling rate. His approximate age for the Earth was one-tenth of today's estimate.

1908
Frank Taylor developed a scientific explanation for continental drift.

1912
Alfred Wegener suggested a version of the modern theory of plate tectonics, which causes continental drift.

1956
Clair Patterson determined from amounts of radioactivity in rocks that the Earth is 4,500 million years old, today's accepted age being nearer 4,600 million.

1960s
Scientists came to accept Weneger's basic ideas and developed the modern version of plate tectonics.

1989
The first of the 24 operational *NAVSTAR* satellites was launched that from the 1990s would provide the GPS, Global Positioning System, to locate any spot on Earth's surface with a few feet.

THE MOON

A moon, also called a *satellite*, is a natural object of reasonable size going around a planet. The one human beings call the *Moon* is Earth's single moon. It has also been known to scientists as *Luna*. The word *luna* comes from the Latin word for *moon*. Seen from Earth, the Moon is about the same size as the Sun. It appears to change shape during its 29.5-day orbit because we can only see the sunlit part of its surface, creating the phases of the Moon. Its pull of gravity also makes the water in seas and oceans rise and fall, calle *tides*.

ORBIT DETAILS

Average distance from Earth
238.866 miles

Average distance from Earth
0.0026 AU (Earth = 1)

Closest distance to Earth (perigee) 225,630 miles

Farthest distance from Sun (aphelion) 252,101 miles

Average orbital speed
0.63 miles per second

Slowest orbital speed
0.6 miles per second

Fastest orbital speed
0.67 miles per second

Time for one orbit
(Earth units) 29 days 12 hours 44 minutes

Axial rotation period
(Earth units) 27 days 7 hours 43 minutes

MOON PROFILE

Diameter at Equator **2160 miles**

Surface area **14.6 million sq miles**

Tilt of axis **1.5°**

Mass (Earth = 1) **0.074**

Volume (Earth = 1) **0.020**

Overall density **3.34 g per cm³**

Gravity (Earth = 1) **0.165**

Number of moons **None**

An artist's illustration of the Moon.

LUNATICS

The Moon features greatly in many legends and stories. One superstition was that if a person stared at the full moon for too long, he or she would become mad. This is where the word *lunatic* comes from. Another legend was that at full moons, certain people would grow hair, long teeth, claws, and become savage and deadly werewolves.

ORIGIN

It is thought the Moon was formed when a huge piece of rock the size of Mars, crashed into Earth around 4.5 billion years ago. Earth was about 100 million yeas old at the time. The loose matter and debris orbiting Earth after the impact came together to form the Moon.

MAJOR FEATURES

The moon has been visited and mapped several times.

Largest Crater
The largest known crater in the solar system, the South Pole-Aitken Basin is 1,398 miles across and 8 miles deep.

Sea of Tranquility
The site for the first *Apollo* Moon landing in 1969. 373 by 559 miles.

Sea of Serenity
Site for the last Moon landing in 1972, about 342 miles wide.

Sea of Crises
Main dark circular area near the top edge, as seen from Earth.

Apennine Mountains
Peaks more than 14,764 feet high.

Copernicus
Small crater (below) but 9,843 feet deep.

Ocean of Storms
Largest lowland plain, covering 2.3 million sq miles.

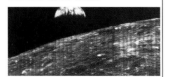

The heavily pitted Copernicus crater.

• See page 55 for information on MOON PROBES.

SURFACE CONDITIONS

ATMOSPHERE:
Tiny traces of helium, neon, hydrogen, and argon

NATURE OF SURFACE:
Craters, mountains, valleys, and plains, called *seas*

AVERAGE SURFACE TEMPERATURE:
-9.39°F

LOWEST SURFACE TEMPERATURE:
-382°F

HIGHEST SURFACE TEMPERATURE: 250°F

WEATHER OR CLIMATE: None

SEASONAL CHANGES: None

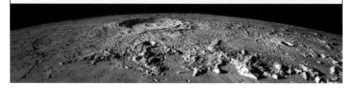

The barren surface of the Moon.

OTHER GEOGRAPHICAL FEATURES

- **MARIA** Meaning *seas*, these are dark lowland plains of hardened basalt rocks which once flowed as lava. They are totally dry, like the rest of the Moon, and occur mainly on the near side.

- **MARE** Dark lowland plains of hardened basalt rocks.

- **RILL** an ancient lava channel, such as the Hyginus Rill and the Hadley Rill.

- **NAMES** Most lunar features are named after famous scientists, especially astronomers.

NEAR AND FAR

- The Moon turns around once in the same time it takes to go around the Earth once.

- This means that it keeps the same side facing Earth.

- Due to the Moon's slight variations in orbit, almost three-fifths of its surface is visible from Earth.

- The other two-fifths is always hidden and has only been seen by spacecraft in lunar orbit.

- The far side is sometimes called the *dark side of the Moon,* but it receives sunlight in the same pattern as the near side.

PHASES OF THE MOON

The Sun lights up only half the Moon at a time. As the Moon moves around the Earth, we see varying amounts of the sunlit half of the Moon. This causes it to show changes of shape, called *phases*.

When the Moon is between the Sun and the Earth, its dark side is turned toward us, and normally, we cannot see it. This is called the *New Moon*. As the Moon moves around the Earth, the sunlit side begins to show. First we see a thin crescent, then a *Half Moon*, and then a *Full Moon*. At Full Moon, all of the sunlit side faces us. After Full Moon, the phase slowly decreases to half and back to a crescent as we see less and less of the sunlit side. Finally, it is New Moon once again. The time from one New Moon to the next New Moon is 29.53 days.

THE MOON AND TIDES

Tides are the regular rising and falling of the surface of the oceans. Although the Sun has some influence, ocean tides are mainly caused by the gravitational interaction between the Earth and the Moon. The gravitational pull from the Moon causes the oceans to bulge in the direction of the Moon. Another bulge occurs on the opposite side, since the Earth is also being pulled toward the Moon and away

from the water on the far side. Since the Earth is spinning on its axis, tides rise and fall twice a day, with the interval between low and high tide being just over six hours.

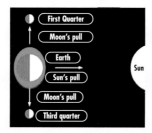

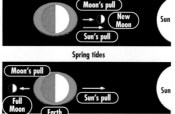

ECLIPSES

Solar eclipse
When the Moon comes between the Earth and Sun and blocks out part, *partial eclipse,* or all, *total eclipse,* of the Sun. The amount of the Sun blocked out varies with the position on Earth. The area of shadow on Earth of a total eclipse is 270 km wide and moves across the Earth as the Earth spins and the Moon continues its orbit. On average, there are 2 total eclipses every 3 years.

Lunar eclipse
When the Earth comes between the Sun and Moon. The Moon seems to fade, but stays a copper-red color, due to sunlight rays bent around the edge of the Earth by the atmosphere.

1959
Russian space probe *Luna 2* crashed into the surface in September—the first human-made object to reach another world. Next month, *Luna 3* went around the Moon and sent back the first images of the previously unknown far side.

1966
Luna 9 soft-landed and sent back the first close-up images of the Moon's surface. *Luna 10* became the first probe to go into Moon orbit.

1966
The first of the US *Surveyor* missions touched down in June and sent back more than 11,000 images.

1968
In December, US *Apollo 8* went into Moon orbit, but did not land, and came back to Earth as practice for the actual landings later.

1969
Apollo 11 touched down on July 20, carrying the first humans to visit another world. Neil Armstrong was first to step out of the *Lunar Module* onto the surface, followed by Edwin "Buzz" Aldrin. Michael Collins stayed on board the command module in lunar orbit.

1969
Apollo 12 landed to carry out scientific studies in November.

1971
Apollo 14 collected 95 pounds of Moon rocks in February.

1972
Apollo 16 collected almost 224 pounds of Moon material.

1972
Eugene Cernan was the last person to step on the Moon.

1994
The *Clementine* space probe collects information that suggestions there might be frozen water on the Moon.

2003
European spacecraft *Smart 1* launched.

2004
In February, President George W. Bush announced plans for a new series to Moon missions.

2004
Smart 1 entered lunar orbit on November 15 to study and map the surface using X-rays.

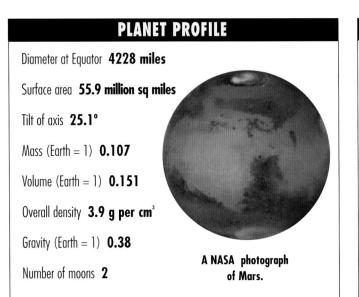

MARS

Named after the Roman god of war, Mars is also called the *Red Planet*, because its surface rocks and dust contain large amounts of the substance *iron oxide*, also known as *rust*. Like Earth, Mars has polar ice caps, volcanoes, canyons, winds, and swirling dust storms. Features resembling river beds and shorelines suggest that great rivers, probably of water, once flowed across Mars' surface. Despite many visits by space probes, landers, and rovers, there are no signs of life.

SURFACE CONDITIONS

ATMOSPHERE:
Mostly carbon dioxide, small amounts of nitrogen and argon, traces of oxygen, carbon monoxide, and water vapor

NATURE OF SURFACE:
Rocks and dust, including giant volcanoes, deep canyons, and dusty plains

AVERAGE SURFACE TEMPERATURE:
-81.4°F

LOWEST SURFACE TEMPERATURE:
-220°F

HIGHEST SURFACE TEMPERATURE:
68°F

WEATHER OR CLIMATE: Clouds, fog, strong winds, dust storms, and a red sky

SEASONAL CHANGES:
Marked (similar to Earth) with intensely cold winters.

A photograph of the surface of Mars taken by the Viking lander.

PLANET PROFILE

Diameter at Equator **4228 miles**

Surface area **55.9 million sq miles**

Tilt of axis **25.1°**

Mass (Earth = 1) **0.107**

Volume (Earth = 1) **0.151**

Overall density **3.9 g per cm^3**

Gravity (Earth = 1) **0.38**

Number of moons **2**

A NASA photograph of Mars.

ORBIT DETAILS

Average distance from Sun
141.6 million miles

Average distance from Sun
1.52 AU (Earth = 1)

**Closest distance to Sun
(perihelion)** 96.22 million miles

**Farthest distance from Sun
(aphelion)** 128.38 million miles

Average orbital speed
14.99 miles per second

Slowest orbital speed
13.6 miles per second

Fastest orbital speed
26.5 m per second

Time for one orbit
(Mars year) 686.9 Earth days

Axial rotation period
(Mars day) 24.62 Earth hours

Sun

Mars

MAJOR FEATURES

North Polar Cap
- Water ice that remains through summer.
- Sand dunes formed by wind.
- North polar cap is about 680 miles across.

South Polar Cap
- The polar frost contains frozen carbon dioxide.
- Carbon dioxide freezes at around -193°F.
- South polar cap is about 260 miles across.

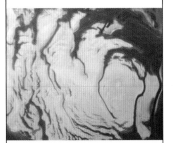

April 2000

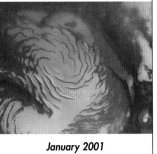

January 2001

MARS MAPS AND PHYSICAL FEATURES

THARSIS MONTES
- Largest volcanic region
- 2,400 miles across
- 6 miles high
- 12 large volcanoes

THARSIS THOLUS
- Partially buried volcano
- 100 mile diameter crater

VALLES MARINERIS
- A vast canyon
- 2,500 miles long
- 4 miles deep in places
- See page 19
  THE GRAND CANYON

ARSIA MONS
- Largest crater in Tharsis Montes
- 75 mile diameter crater

ELYSIUM PLANITIA
- Second largest volcanic region
- 1000 miles by 1440 miles

OLYMPUS MONS
- Largest volcano in solar system
- Nearly 15 miles high
- Taller than three Mt. Everests
- Very flat —typical slopes 2° to 5°

CYDONIA MENSAE (the face)
- Natural landform resembling a giant face
- First photographed by *Viking 1* on 7/25/76
- Image represents an area 2.2 miles by 1 mile

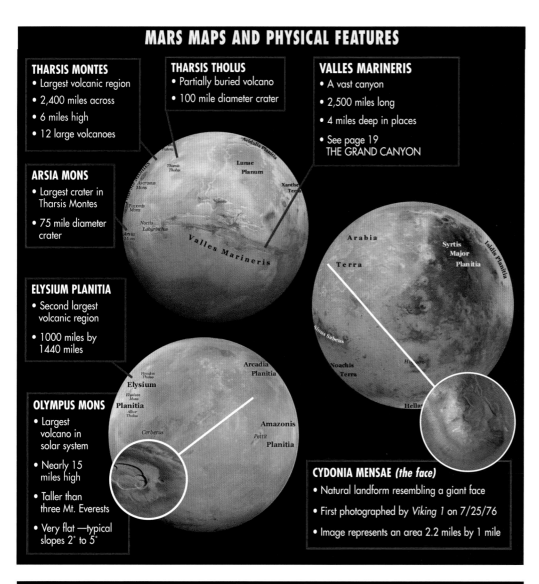

MARS TIMELINE

4,000 years ago
Ancient Egyptian astronomers observe Mars.

3,000 years ago
The Babylonians called Mars *Nirgal*, the *Star of Death*.

1610
Mars is studied by Galileo with his early telescope.

1877
Giovanni Schiaparelli produced maps and written studies of Mars. Mars' two moons were discovered by Asaph Hall.

1964
Mariner 4 is the first craft to reach Mars and returned with 21 pictures.

1969
Mariners 6 and *7* flew past, sending 175 close-up pictures, as two more Russian probes failed.

1971
Mariner 9 took over 7,300 close-up picture of the Martian surface.

1976
US *Vikings 1* and *2* landed in June and August, carried out many observations.

1997
Mars Global Surveyor entered Mars orbit and still operating in 2005.

1997
Mars Pathfinder lands and its rover, *Sojourner*, explored surface .

1999
The US *Mars Climate Orbiter* and *Mars Polar Lander* reached the planet, but both fell silent.

2001
US *Mars Odyssey* successfully reached Mars orbit and has sent back a wealth of scientific information.

2003
European *Mars Express* entered orbit but its *Beagle 2* lander was lost.

2004
Mars exploration rovers *Spirit* and *Opportunity* touched down and began to explore the Martian surface and send back a wealth of information.

2005
Spirit and *Opportunity* continue to explore and send back data.

2020
Proposed end date for possible US missions carrying astronauts to Mars.

MARTIANS!

- Giovanni Schiaparelli's studies of Mars in 1877 used the term *canali*, meaning *channels*, which could be naturally occurring.

- Some people took this to mean *canals* made by some advanced life-form, like on Earth.

- Percival Lowell developed the idea to suggest Martians dug canals to take water from the planet's ice-caps to water their crops, since other areas on Mars changed color with the seasons.

- The myth of Martians began, and H. G. Wells featured their invasion of Earth in *War of the Worlds* in 1898. It continues to be popular today.

- The channels are now known to be imagined or perhaps long-dry watercourses, and the color changes are probably dust storms.

> • See pages 55 for information on space probes to Mars.

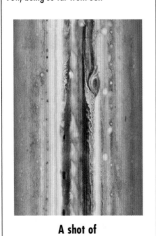

JUPITER

Jupiter is by far the biggest planet in the solar system. It is a vast planet of swirling gases and storms of unimaginable fury. As the fifth planet out, it is the nearest *gas giant*, a planet made almost completely of gases, to the Sun. It is not much smaller than some of the stars called *brown dwarfs*. Jupiter does not shine itself, but reflects sunlight as all planets do. Even so, its huge pull of gravity holds more than 60 moons in orbit around it. Jupiter is named after the Roman king of the gods, also called *Jove*.

ATMOSPHERIC CONDITIONS

ATMOSPHERE:
Mostly hydrogen, some helium, traces of methane, water vapor, ammonia, hydrogen sulphide, and other gases

NATURE OF SURFACE:
Visible surface is whirling gases, possibly a solid surface on a small rocky core miles below visible surface

AVERAGE CLOUD-TOP SURFACE TEMP: -202°F

LOWEST CLOUD-TOP SURFACE TEMP: -261°F

HIGHEST CLOUD-TOP SURFACE TEMP: -277°F

WEATHER OR CLIMATE:
Complete cloud coverage with storms and wind speeds up to 272.84 mph.

SEASONAL CHANGES:
Few, being so far from Sun

A shot of Jupiter's atmosphere.

PLANET PROFILE

Diameter at Equator **88,850 miles**

Surface area **33.7 billion sq miles**

Tilt of axis **3.13°**

Mass (Earth = 1) **318**

Volume (Earth = 1) **1,236**

Overall density **1.33 g per cm³**

Gravity (Earth = 1) **2.36**

Number of moons **more than 60**

A NASA photograph of Jupiter.

ORBIT DETAILS

Average distance from Sun
483.6 million miles

Average distance from Sun
5.203 AU (Earth = 1)

**Closest distance to Sun
(perihelion)** 460.27 million miles

**Farthest distance from Sun
(aphelion)** 507.12 million miles

Average orbital speed
8.07 miles per second

Slowest orbital speed
7.7 miles per second

Fastest orbital speed
8.5 miles per second

Time for one orbit
(Jupiter year) 11.87 Earth years

Axial rotation period
(Jupiter day) 9.92 Earth days

Sun

Jupiter

MAJOR FEATURES

Jupiter has several distinctive features mapped by astronomers.

Great Red Spot
A giant storm system three times wider than Earth, that travels around Jupiter just south of the equator, once every 6 days.

White Spot
Smaller circulatory storm systems in Jupiter's atmosphere, about the size of Earth.

Browns Spots
Stormy regions that are probably warmer than surrounding clouds.

Rings
These consist of dust knocked from Jupiter's moons by meteor strikes.

Inner Structure
Central small rocky core, then a layer of "metallic" hydrogen, then liquid hydrogen, and finally the outermost atmosphere of mainly hydrogen gas. These layers flow from one to another, with no sharp boundaries.

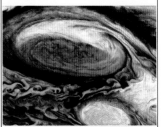

Jupiter's Giant Red Spot.

• See page 55 for information on probes to Jupiter.

OTHER FEATURES

- **BELTS** Strips of dark clouds that wind from west to east (left to right) and change through the years.

- **ZONES** Lengths of light-colored clouds that change like the darker belts. Blue-tinted clouds are the lowest and warmest. Zones contain higher clouds than belts.

- **TURBULENCE** Belts sometimes move in the opposite direction to their neighboring zones, creating swirling patterns of storms and turbulence along their edges.

MOON RECORDS

- Ganymede is the largest moon in the solar system.

- Callisto is the most heavily cratered object.

- Io probably has the most volcanic activity.

NASA images showing IO volcanoes produce red- and black-colored lava flows and yellow sulphur patches.

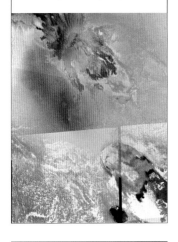

JUPITER'S RINGS

- **MAIN RING** Dust from Adrastea and Metis moons.
- **FIRST GOSSAMER RING** Dust from Thebe moon.
- **SECOND GOSSAMER RING** Dust from Amalthea moon.
- **FAINT OUTER RING**

TRUE GIANT

Jupiter has more than twice as much mass than all the other eight planets added together. However, it would probably need to be 50 times heavier to start burning like a true star.

SPEED SPIN

Jupiter is not only the largest planet, it also spins around the fastest, once in less than 10 Earth hours. The spinning speed of the upper atmosphere at the equator is 5 minutes faster than at the poles, so the atmosphere is continually being twisted and torn.

JUPITER'S MOONS

On January 7–11, 1610, Galileo discovered Jupiter's four main moons, now known as *Galilean moons*, by following their orbits across the face of the planet.

This was direct evidence that the Earth was not at the center of everything. It also strengthened his idea that planets like Earth and Jupiter probably revolved around the Sun.

MOON (or group)	DIAMETER	DISTANCE FROM JUPITER
Inner group	Four small moons less than 125 miles across	Less than 136,702 miles
Io	2,263 miles	124,280 miles
Europa	1,1939 miles	262,044 miles
Ganymede	3,270 miles	664,818 miles
Callisto	2,995 miles	1,169,475 miles
Themisto	4.97 miles	4,592,146 miles
Himalia group	Most under 62.14 miles	6.8–7.5 milllion miles
Ananke group	Most under 62.14 miles	13 million miles
Carme group	Most under 62.14 miles	14 million miles
Pasiphaë	Small outermost moons	14 million miles

JUPITER TIMELINE

3,000 years ago
Jupiter was known to Greeks and then the Romans.

1,500 years ago
In Ancient China, Jupiter was known as the *Wood Star*.

1610
Galileo observed Jupiter's four largest moons.

1665
The Great Red Spot was first observed.

1690
Giovanni Domenico Cassini noticed that the upper atmosphere takes longer to spin at the poles than around the equator.

1973
US *Pioneer 10* probe flew past.

1979
Voyager 1 flew past taking spectacular photographs. *Voyager 2* achieved similar results.

1992
Ulysses probe passes by Jupiter on its way to the Sun, taking measurements.

1994
Parts of comet *Shoemaker-Levy 9* hit Jupiter in July, photographed by the approaching *Galileo* space probe.

1995
Galileo became the first probe to orbit Jupiter on December 7. On the same day, an atmosphere probe it had already released parachuted 94 miles into the atmosphere, collecting information for almost one hour.

1996–2003
Galileo continued its studies of Jupiter and its nearer moons, flying past many of them several times.

2000
The Great Red Spot had shrunk to about half its size in 1900.

2000
Cassini probe passes on way to Saturn.

2003
Galileo plunged into the clouds in September.

2007
The *New Horizons* probe is due to fly past, on its way to Pluto.

2010
The US Jupiter probe *Juno* is scheduled for launch. *Juno* will orbit over Jupiter's poles.

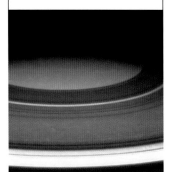

SATURN

Known for its glistening, breathtakingly beautiful rings, Saturn is the solar system's second-largest planet after its neighbor, Jupiter. Saturn was the Roman god of farming, civilization, prosperity, and also the name of the rockets that powered the *Apollo* astronauts to the Moon. Due to its fast spin, gas giant make-up, and very light weight compared to its size, Saturn bulges around its equator as it rotates. This means the planet is 7,456 miles wider than it is tall.

ATMOSPHERIC CONDITIONS

ATMOSPHERE:
Mostly hydrogen, small amount of helium, traces of methane, water vapor, and ammonia

NATURE OF SURFACE:
Visible surface is whirling gases, possibly a solid surface on a rocky core miles below visible surface

AVERAGE CLOUD-TOP SURFACE TEMPERATURE: -202°F

LOWEST CLOUD-TOP SURFACE TEMPERATURE: -331.6°F

HIGHEST CLOUD-TOP SURFACE TEMPERATURE: -184°F

WEATHER OR CLIMATE:
Clouds and storms of fast-moving gases, high wind speeds

SEASONAL CHANGES:
Few, being so far from Sun

Saturn's northern hemisphere is presently a serene blue, much like that of Uranus or Neptune.

PLANET PROFILE

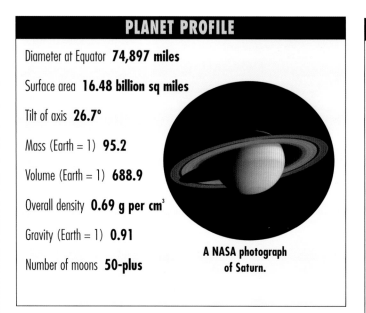

Diameter at Equator **74,897 miles**

Surface area **16.48 billion sq miles**

Tilt of axis **26.7°**

Mass (Earth = 1) **95.2**

Volume (Earth = 1) **688.9**

Overall density **0.69 g per cm³**

Gravity (Earth = 1) **0.91**

Number of moons **50-plus**

A NASA photograph of Saturn.

ORBIT DETAILS

Average distance from Sun
806 million miles

Average distance from Sun
9.54 AU (Earth = 1)

Closest distance to Sun (perihelion) 838 million miles

Farthest distance from Sun (aphelion) 940 million miles

Average orbital speed
5.96 miles per second

Slowest orbital speed
5.66 miles per second

Fastest orbital speed
6.28 miles per second

Time for one orbit
(Saturn year) 29.46 Earth years

Axial rotation period
(Saturn day) 10.77 Earth hours

Sun

Saturn

MAJOR FEATURES

Saturn has been explored by a number of probes.

Rings
These are made of billions of fragments of ice and rock which reflect sunlight, glisten and sparkle. The largest particles are the size of a car.

- Fainter, more distant rings
- Outermost main ring A
- Middle ring B
- Innermost main ring C
- Innermost ring D
- Cassini Division
- Encke Division

Equatorial Zone
Rotates about 25 minutes faster per Saturn day than the Temperate Zones, and has wider cloud banding.

North Temperate Zone
Clouds and winds of 1,118 mph.

South Temperate Zone
Lighter colored clouds and a warm dark spot.

Saturn's poles are shown in this NASA image.

OTHER FEATURES

- **CORE** Saturn's core is probably very hot, nearly 12,000°C, and the planet gives out more heat than it receives from the Sun.

- **SOUTH POLE** A very hot region that glows bright on infrared photographs.

- **BAND CLOUDS** Less obvious than Jupiter's, consisting of stripes and zones of clouds at different temperatures. They tend to be wider nearer the equator.

- **WHITE SPOTS** Tend to come and go, probably areas of swirling gases.

MAIN MOONS

After Titan, the second to fifth moons discovered for Saturn were observed by Giovanni Domenico Cassini.

YEAR	MOON	DIAMETER	DISTANCE
1684	Tethys	659 miles	183,056 miles
1684	Dione	696 miles	234,505 miles
1672	Rhea	951 miles	327,525 miles
1671	Iapetus	892 miles	2,212,081 miles

TITAN

A selection of shots of Titan from the European Southern Observatory.

- Titan is the second-largest moon in the solar system, behind Jupiter's Ganymede.

- Titan has a thick atmosphere.

- Its atmosphere is mainly nitrogen (like Earth's), plus methane, ethane, acetylene, propane, carbon dioxide, carbon monoxide, hydrogen cyanide, and helium.

THE RINGS OF SATURN

The rings of Saturn were first noticed by Galileo, who could not quite make them out with his early telescope. He guessed they might be Moons, one on each side, and called them "Ears of Saturn."
They appear to change in shape when viewed from Earth, as they are tilted and slowly turn with Saturn's orbit, so we see them at different angles. Viewed edge-on, they are at their thinnest, about every 15 years. Each main ring is made of thousands of smaller 'ringlets'.

Name	Inner edge distance from Saturn (miles)	Width (miles)
D Ring	3,726	4,440
C Ring	9,010	10,874
Columbo Gap	11,060	62.14
Maxwell Gap	17,088	167.7
B Ring	19,884	15,835
Cassini Division	35,728	2,920
A Ring	38,649	9,072
Encke Division	45,714	202
F Ring	49,834	314
G Ring	64,584	4,971
E Ring	74,565	186,420

• See page 10 for information on GALILEO GALILEI.

VAST BUT LIGHT

Saturn is the only planet whose density, or mass per volume, is less than water. If there were a tank of water big enough to hold it, Saturn would float.

2,500 years ago
Saturn was known to Greeks and then the Romans.

1610
Galileo saw two shapes on either side of Saturn, the first observations of its rings.

1655
Christiaan Huygens discovered Titan and gave explaination of Saturn's ring system.

1789
William Herschel discovered that Saturn bulges at the equator and flattens at the poles.

1847
John Herschel named the known seven moons of Saturn.

1979
Pioneer was the first space probe to visit Saturn.

1980
Voyager 1 sent back the first clear pictures of the planet.

1981
Voyager 2 flew past in August and discovered further features, including darker "spoke" regions in Saturn's B ring (not seen since by Cassini), smaller gaps between rings, and more moons in close-up.

1997
Cassini-Huygens space probe launched on October 15.

2004
Cassini-Huygens flew close to the moon *Phoebe* in June and reached Saturn orbit on July 1.

2004
After two Titan flybys, the *Huygens* lander was released from the *Cassini orbiter* on December 25.

2005
Huygens plunged into Titan's atmosphere on January 14, sending information after touching down. *Cassini* continued to orbit and fly past many moons, especially Titan.

2008
Expected end of the main mission for *Cassini orbiter*, but the mission may be extended.

URANUS

Uranus is the third gas giant and seventh planet from the Sun. It is very similar in size and structure to Neptune, being partly gas, but also containing much rocky and frozen material. The axis of Uranus is almost at right angles to the Sun. Some scientists believe an Earth-sized object crashed into Uranus soon after it was created, giving it its unique axis. The planet is named after the Greek god of the heavens, who was also the father of Saturn.

ATMOSPHERIC CONDITIONS

ATMOSPHERE:
Mostly hydrogen, about one-sixth helium, also methane, and traces of ammoni

NATURE OF SURFACE:
Gassy, with any solid surface deep below; glows in sunlight as bright blue-green or cyan

AVERAGE CLOUD-TOP SURFACE TEMP: -337°F

LOWEST CLOUD-TOP SURFACE TEMP: -353.2°F

HIGHEST CLOUD-TOP SURFACE TEMP: -328°F

WEATHER OR CLIMATE:
Swirling clouds, winds, and gases, despite smooth, "glassy" appearance

SEASONAL CHANGES:
Extreme, since Uranus lies on its side so that during each orbit, both poles and the equatorial regions face the Sun.

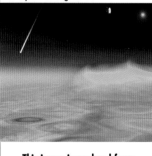

This image is rendered from the clouds of Uranus, with the *Voyager* spacecraft seen in the sky above.

PLANET PROFILE

Diameter at Equator **31,763.25 miles**

Surface area **3.118 billion sq miles**

Tilt of axis **97.8° (almost at a right angle to the Sun)**

Mass (Earth = 1) **14.54**

Volume (Earth = 1) **63.1**

Overall density **1.32 g per cm³**

Gravity (Earth = 1) **0.89**

Number of moons **approaching 30 and counting**

A NASA photograph of Uranus.

ORBIT DETAILS

Average distance from Sun
1,783 million miles

Average distance from Sun
19.2 AU (Earth = 1)

Closest distance to Sun (perihelion) 1,699 million miles

Farthest distance from Sun (aphelion) 1,868 million miles

Average orbital speed
4.22 miles per second

Slowest orbital speed
4.15 miles per second

Fastest orbital speed
4.43 miles per second

Time for one orbit
(Uranus year) 84.1 Earth years

Axial rotation period
(Uranus day) 17.24 Earth hours

Sun

Uranus

MAJOR FEATURES

Uranus has been mapped from Earth and the *Voyager* probe.

Inner Structure
Uranus is probably quite similar in composition all the way through, with gases and particles of rocks and ice intermingled.

Color
Uranus usually appears pale to mid blue-green, a color known as *cyan*, probably because methane crystals in its atmosphere absorb most of the red light in sunlight, leaving it mostly blue.

Streaking
Hubble Space telescope images reveal faint streaks that slowly change, perhaps due to seasonal variations.

Warmer Equator
Despite Uranus's extreme tilt, the equator is slightly warmer than the polar regions.

An artist's impression of the rings of Uranus.

OTHER FEATURES

- **SURFACE FEATURES**
  There are few obvious features when Uranus is viewed through telescopes from Earth. the surface appears to be smooth with a "satin" glow.

- **MAGNETIC FIELD**
  This invisible field's center is not in the center of the planet. It is tilted at 60° compared to the planet's spinning axis.

ON ITS SIDE

Due to Uranus' axis tilt, the planet spins as if lying on its side, rolling around the Sun. The axis of Uranus does not move as it orbits the Sun.

The southern pole of Uranus (pointing sideways) faces the Sun for a short time. Then, as the orbit continues, the northern pole gradually comes around to face the Sun, in the opposite part of the orbit.

MAIN MOONS

MOON	DIAMETER	DISTANCE
Miranda	293 miles	80,703 miles
Ariel	719 miles	118,631 miles
Umbriel	727 miles	165,292 miles
Titania	980 miles	271,117 miles
Oberon	964 miles	362,599 miles

There are about 14 smaller moons inside Miranda's orbit. The largest of those is Puck, whose diameter is 99 miles across.

RINGS OF URANUS

Ring	Distance from center of Uranus (miles)	Width of ring (miles)
1986U2R	23,612	1,553
6	25,998	0.62–1.86
5	26,240	1.24–1.86
4	26,458	1.24–1.86
Alpha	27,788	2.4–6.2
Beta	28,378	4.35–7.46
Eta	29,323	0–1.24
Gamma	29,596	0.62–2.49
Delta	30,006	1.86–5.59
Lamda	31,081	0.62–1.24
Epsilon	31,777	12.43–62.14

ODD LITTLE WORLD

- Uranus's innermost principal moon, Miranda, has one of the oddest appearances in the solar system.

- Massive canyons scar the surface, as well as mountains, cliffs, and craters.

- Three huge race-track-like shapes, called *ovoids*, are prominent, perhaps formed by rocks being pushed up from within.

- Miranda's Verona Rupes is a huge fault scarp. At 12.4 miles high, it is the highest cliff in the solar system.

- There are also many smaller grooves on Miranda that look like aerial pictures of strip mines on Earth.

- Miranda may have frozen water, methane-type substances, and rocks on its surface.

A composite image of Uranus's moon Miranda.

• *See pages 18–19 for information on Earth.*

• See pages 18–19 for information on Earth.

URANUS TIMELINE

Ancient times
Uranus may have been known to ancient people.

1690
John Flamsteed recorded Uranus as a dim star-like object, *34 Tauri*.

1748
James Bradley observed Uranus as a faint star. He also saw it in 1750 and 1753.

1764
Pierre Charles Le Monnier recorded Uranus a dozen times from this year to 1771.

1781
William Herschel discovered Uranus.

1787
William Herschel discovered moons *Titania* and *Oberon*.

1851
William Lassell discovered Ariel and Umbriel, Uranus's second- and third-nearest "twin moons," on October 24.

1948
Gerard Kuiper discovered Miranda, Uranus's innermost moon, on February 16.

1977
Voyager 2 was lauched on its journey across the solar system.

1977
In March, a system of rings was suspected as the planet blocked out a faint star behind it in an odd manner.

1982
Voyager 2 passed Uranus, at the time when its south pole pointed directly towards the Sun.

1986
Voyager 2 made its closest flypast on January 24, 68,350 miles from its surface. It saw the rings in detail and discovered an extra one, also 10 more moons in addition to the five visible from Earth with telescopes.

2007
The Sun will be overhead at the equator of Uranus, midway between its apparent journey from being directly over one pole to overhead at the other pole.

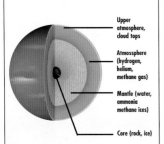
NEPTUNE

Neptune's deep blue color of the fourth gas giant inspired its name, the Roman god of the sea. Neptune's atmosphere is ravaged by the fastest winds in the solar system. Although it is the fourth largest planet, it is third heaviest, being denser than its neighbor, Uranus. Also like Uranus, Neptune's atmosphere probably extends about one-fifth of the way toward the center. Then, it gives way to a mix of semi-liquid ice, rocks, methane, and ammonia, with a central core of maily partly molten rocks and metals.

ATMOSPHERIC CONDITIONS

ATMOSPHERE:
Mostly hydrogen, one-fifth helium, traces of methane and ethane

NATURE OF SURFACE:
Gassy, with incredibly fast wind

AVERAGE CLOUD-TOP SURFACE TEMP: -364°F

LOWEST CLOUD-TOP SURFACE TEMP: -369.4°F

HIGHEST CLOUD-TOP SURFACE TEMP: -360.4°F

WEATHER OR CLIMATE:
Storms and swirling gases move at 1,243 mph, more than four times faster than Earth's fastest winds in tornadoes

SEASONAL CHANGES:
Neptune has few seasonal changes. Since it is so far from the Sun, solar heat and light have little effect on this cold planet.

Upper atmosphere, cloud tops

Atmossphere (hydrogen, helium, methane gas)

Mantle (water, ammonia methane ices)

Core (rock, ice)

PLANET PROFILE

Diameter at Equator **30,775 miles**

Surface area **2.94 billion sq miles**

Tilt of axis **28.3°**

Mass (Earth = 1) **17.15**

Volume (Earth = 1) **57.7**

Overall density **1.64 g per cm³**

Gravity (Earth = 1) **1.14**

Number of moons **about 13**

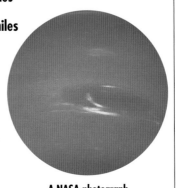

A NASA photograph of Neptune. The great dark spot is in the center.

ORBIT DETAILS

Average distance from Sun
2,795 million miles

Average distance from Sun
30.1 AU (Earth = 1)

Closest distance to Sun (perihelion) 2,271 million miles

Farthest distance from Sun (aphelion) 2,819 million miles

Average orbital speed
3.38 miles per second

Slowest orbital speed
3.35 miles km per second

Fastest orbital speed
3.41 miles per second

Time for one orbit
(Neptune year) 164.8 Earth years

Axial rotation period
(Neptune day) 16.1 Earth hours

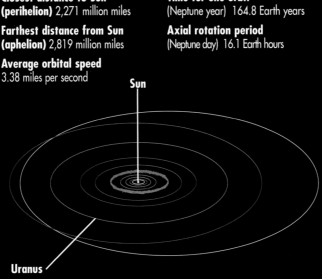

Sun

Uranus

MAJOR FEATURES

Neptune has been mapped from Earth and by probes.

Great Dark Spot
About as wide is Earth, this was probably a vast storm system of swirling gases in the northern hemisphere. It faded in the mid 1990s but another similar area, GDS2, appeared.

Color
Neptune is a dark blue-green, probably because methane crystals in its atmosphere absorbs the red light in sunlight, leaving it mainly blue.

Winds
Neptune has some of the fastest winds in the solar system, blasting along at over 1,430 mph.

Inner Structure
Outer atmosphere of hydrogen and helium, then lower down more methane and ammonia, with more rock particles, merging into melted rock and metal in the central core.

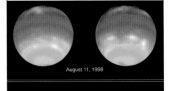
August 11, 1998

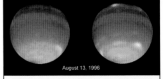
August 13, 1996

Storms rage on Neptune during 1998.

OTHER FEATURES

- **MAGNETIC FIELD** Tilted at 47° to Neptune's axis. Also off center from the middle of the planet by more than 8,078 miles.

- **OUTER CLOUDS** Some clouds high above the main cloud layer cast shadows on those below, such as Earth's clouds cast shadows on the land.

- **RINGS** About 9 faint rings surround Neptune, with a strange structure showing clumps of larger material rather than spread-out small particles.

- **ARCS** Curved arcs within the outermost ring, called *Adams*, are probably due to the movements and gravity of the moon Galatea on their inner side.

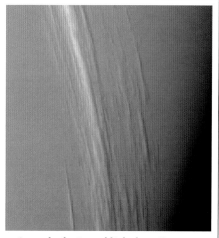

Outer clouds pictured high above Neptune.

THE FIRST PAPER PLANET

Neptune was the first planet to be discovered on paper. Calculations of the orbit of Uranus showed that another body beyond it affects Uranus'movements (see TIMELINE, 1846).

NAMING NEPTUNE

- Various experts, including Arago, proposed *Leverrier* after its co-discoverer.

- Others propoesed *Poseidon* (right), Greek sea god.

- Galle proposed *Janus*.

- Challis suggested *Oceanus*.

- Le Verrier himself proposed *Neptune*.

- The name *Neptune* was adopted by the end of 1846.

NEPTUNE'S RINGS

These are very faint, difficult to measure and also seem to change rapidly.

Name	Distance from surface (miles)	Width (miles)
Galle (1989 N3R)	10,625	9.32
Leverrier (1989 N2R)	17,667	9.32
Lassell (1989 N4R)	19,045	3.73
Arago	20,412	not clear
Adams (1989 N1R)	23,705	less than 31
Liberty Arc	leading arc	not known
Equality Arc	middle arc	not known
Fraternity Arc	trailing arc	not known
Courage Arc	n/a	not known

VOYAGER VISIT

- *Voyager 2* is the only probe to visit Neptune and got closest to this planet than any other planet on its journey from Earth.

- It observed Neptune from June to October 1989.

- At its closest on August 25, the probe passed just 3,100 miles above Neptune's northern pole.

- A few hours later it passed within 24,850 miles of Neptune's largest moon, Triton.

- Triton was *Voyager 2*'s last studied object before it left the solar system.

SIZE AND SHAPE

Neptune is the fourth biggest planet in size, slightly wider than Uranus. But because Neptune is more dense than Uranus, it is the third heaviest planet after Jupiter and Saturn.

1612
Galileo saw Neptune on December 28. He didn't recoginize it as a planet.

1843
John Adams calculated that another planet farther out than Uranus was probably affecting its orbit.

1846
In the spring, a series of messages and calculations between Urbain Le Verrier, John Herschel, James Challis and Johann Galle made it clear that there was probably an eighth planet beyond Uranus.

1846
James Challis recorded Neptune twice in August.

1846
Neptune was discovered by Johann Galle and John Adams from Urbain Le Verrier's calculations on September 23.

1846
Neptune's largest moon Triton identified by William Lassell.

1880
Camille Flammarion proposed the name Triton for Neptune's main moon.

1949
Nereid discovered by Gerard Kuiper.

1977
Voyager 2 launched on its journey across the solar system.

1989
The only space probe to visit, *Voyager 2*, flew past on August 25, 12 years after its launch.

1998
The *Neptune Papers*, missing documents from the Royal Greenwich Observatory, were found and further evidence came to light about who actually calculated the position of Neptune first. Le Verrier was favored, though he didn't actually search for it himself.

2011
Neptune will be in the same position in relation to the Sun as when it was discovered, having completed one orbit.

PLUTO

Pluto has held the honor of being the smallest and farthest planet in the solar system, since its discovery in 1930. However, discoveries in 2003 and 2005 may threaten this record. A tiny, frozen, distant world, Pluto is the least known of all planets. Our information comes from telescopes only, since no space probe has visited it. Pluto also has a highly unusual orbit, being very oval. For part of its immensely long year, Pluto is actually nearer to the Sun than its neighbor, Neptune.

SURFACE CONDITIONS

ATMOSPHERE:
Not clearly known, very thin, probably nitrogen, carbon monoxide, and methane

NATURE OF SURFACE:
Rock and various chemicals frozen as ice

AVERAGE SURFACE TEMPERATURE: -382°F

LOWEST SURFACE TEMPERATURE: -403.6°F

HIGHEST SURFACE TEMPERATURE: -362°F

WEATHER OR CLIMATE
Atmosphere may move as gases when Pluto is closer to the Sun, but then freeze as nitrogen ice at its farthest distance

An artist's impression of the surface of Pluto.

PLANET PROFILE

Diameter at Equator **1,412 miles**

Surface area **6.9 million sq miles**

Tilt of axis **122.5° to its orbit, 115° to orbits of other planets**

Mass (Earth = 1) **0.002**

Volume (Earth = 1) **0.007**

Overall density **1.75 g per cm³**

Gravity (Earth = 1) **0.06**

Number of moons **1**

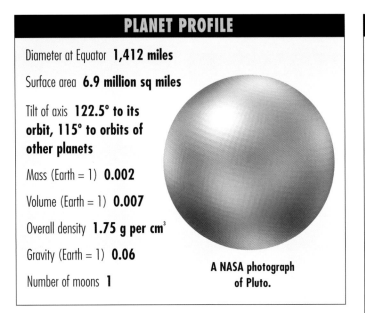

A NASA photograph of Pluto.

ORBIT DETAILS

Average distance from Sun
3,670 million miles

Average distance from Sun
39.5 AU (Earth = 1)

Closest distance to Sun (perihelion) 2,756 million miles

Farthest distance from Sun (aphelion) 4,583 million miles

Average orbital speed
2.9 miles per second

Slowest orbital speed
2.28 miles per second

Fastest orbital speed
3.8 miles per second

Time for one orbit
(Pluto year) 248.1 Earth years

Axial rotation period
(Pluto day) 6.39 Earth days

Sun

Pluto

PLUTO'S MOON

Charon, Pluto's moon, is half the size of Pluto, which makes the pair a double planet system.

- Charon is the largest moon compared to its planet in the solar system.
- It measures 748 miles across, just under half of Pluto's size.
- Charon's orbit distance is 12,117 miles across, and its orbit time is just 6.39 days.
- Charon's spin and orbit time, combined with Pluto's spin, mean that both Pluto and Charon keep the same face toward each other at all times. This is called *tidal locking*.
- Charon's name was officially agreed in 1985.
- This moon has no atmosphere, but its surface is possibly coated in frozen water.

IS PLUTO A TRUE PLANET?

In the 1990s, the debate increased about whether Pluto should be considered a true planet.

REASONS AGAINST

- Very eccentric orbit, with its closest distance to the Sun only 3/5 of the farthest distance.

- Orbit is tilted compared to other planets, whose orbits all lie flat, as if on a giant plate.

- Small size, less than half the diameter of next-smallest planet, Mercury.

- Other objects in the solar system similar in size to Pluto have recently been discovered. Object *2003UB313*, provisionally called *Xena*, is about 1,863 across. If Pluto is a planet, then Xena also should be classed as one.

REASONS FOR

- Pluto is small but much larger than any asteroids in th Asteroid Belt, and one of the largest objects to be discovered in the Kuiper Belt beyond Neptune.

- It has its own moon and an atmosphere.

- It has been established as a planet for over 70 years.

• See pages 34–35 for information on the ASTEROIDS.

An artist's impression of another newly discovered object, *Sedna*.

MANY NAMES

In the week's following Pluto's discovery, known as *Planet X*, by Clyde Tombaugh (left), dozens of names were suggested including:

Artemis, Athene, Atlas, Cosmos, Cronus, Hera, Hercules, Icarus, Idana, Minerva, Odin, Pax, Persephone, Perseus, Prometheus, Tantalus, Vulcan, Zymal

- *Pluto* was first suggested by Venetia Burney, an 11-year-old girl from Oxford, England.

- She suggested it was so cold and distant, it could be named after the Roman god of the underworld.

- Her grandfather mentioned this to an astronomer friend, who contacted the discovery committee in the USA.

- The name *Pluto* was quickly agreed upon.

PLUTINOS

From the 1990s, many smaller bodies have been discovered in the Kuiper Belt past Neptune. These KBOs (Kuiper Belt Objects) are regarded as minor planets, or Plutinos, if they complete two orbits around the Sun in the same time it takes Neptune to make three orbits.

SMALLEST PLANET

Pluto is not only the smallest planet, it is smaller in size than seven moons of some of the giant gas planets Jupiter and Saturn — Ganymede, Titan, Callisto, Io, Europa, and Triton. It is even smaller than the Earth's Moon.

ODD ORBIT

- Pluto has by far the most elliptical orbit of any planet.

- From February 1979 to February 1999, Pluto was closer than Neptune to the Sun.

1902
Percival Lowell predicted another body beyond Neptune.

1915
Lowell made another prediction, this time fairly close to Pluto's actual size and position, but many experts say that was coincidence (see below).

1930
Pluto was discovered by Clyde Tombaugh at the Lowell Observatory, Arizona.

1930
Pluto became the official name on May 30.

1978
Pluto's moon *Charon* was discovered by James Christy.

1977
Voyager 1 was launched and originally was due to visit Pluto, but was redirected to fly past Saturn's moon *Titan*.

1992
From September, hundreds of small, icy objects were discovered beyond Neptune, in a zone now known as the *Kuiper Belt*.

1993
Debates began as to whether Pluto was a true planet or a Kuiper Belt object (see panel).

1995
New calculations showed that Pluto has almost no effect on the orbits of Neptune and Uranus, so its original discovery was largely coincidence.

2001
NASA began to plan and build *New Horizons* space probe.

2006
New Horizons probe planned for launch in January, to visit Pluto, Charon, and objects in the Kuiper Belt.

2015
New Horizons expected to fly within 6,215 miles of Pluto in July, the first craft to visit the planet, and then within 18,641 miles of Charon.

2020 and beyond
New Horizons may encounter objects in the Kuiper Belt.

ASTEROIDS

A steroids are chunks of rock that orbit the Sun. They are pieces of rock left over from the formation of the planets and moons. Most asteroids are too far away and too faint to be seen clearly without a telescope. Most orbit far away, beyond Mars, but occasionally one may come closer to the Sun or Earth. Asteroids have hit the Earth in the past. A major impact about 65 million years ago may be linked to the extinction of the dinosaurs.

ASTEROID TYPES

A stony asteroid

- There are three types of asteroids, each made of different materials.

- More than 90% of all known asteroids are called stony asteroids, because they contain stony materials called *silicates*.

- About another 5–6% of asteroids are made of metal. They contain mostly nickel and iron.

- The rest of the asteroids contain a mixture of silicates and metals.

- Metal asteroids may be from the smashed core of a small planet that was torn apart millions, or billions, of years ago.

- Some asteroids are very dark, because they are covered in carbon compounds.

THE TROJANS

If asteroids stray too close to the giant Jupiter, they can get trapped in its orbit. There are two groups of asteroids that circle around the solar system in front and behind Jupiter. Scientists have named these asteroids the *Trojans*. Sometimes, they fall into Jupiter's gravitational pull and become satellites of Jupiter.

An artists' impression of a Trojan asteroid.

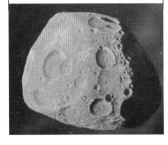

ASTEROID FACTS

Asteroids range in size from dust particles to objects nearly 621 miles across.

- The biggest asteroid, called *Ceres*, is about 580 miles across.

- Ceres was the first asteroid to be discovered. It was found by the Italian astronomer Giuseppe Piazzi in 1801.

- Asteroids spin as they fly through space.

- Large asteroids are tracked in case any of them follow an orbit that may collide with Earth in the future.

- The biggest asteroids are ball-shaped, like small planets, leading to their other names, the *minor planets,* or *planetoids*.

- Astronomers think the two moons of Mars, Phobos and Deimos, may be captured asteroids.

- The Moon's craters were caused by asteroid impacts.

• See page 20 for information on the MOON and its craters.

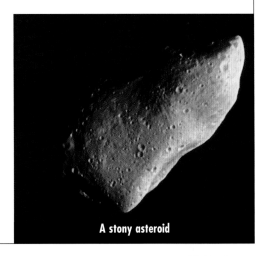

A stony asteroid

WHERE DO ASTEROIDS COME FROM?

- Most asteroids orbit the Sun in a broad band, called the *Asteroid Belt*, between the orbits of Mars and Jupiter.

- The Asteroid Belt marks the end of the inner solar system and the beginning of the outer solar system.

- Asteroids that cross the orbit of Mars are called *Amors asteroids*.

- Asteroids that cross the Earth's orbit are called *Apollos*.

- Atens asteroids have orbits that are inside the Earth's orbit.

- The Trojans are asteroids that orbit ahead of or behind a planet. Mars, Jupiter, and Neptune have Trojan asteroids in their orbits.

- There are also rocky and icy bodies orbiting the Sun further out than Neptune in a region, called the *Kuiper Belt*. These are known as *Kuiper Belt Object* or *Trans-Neptune Objects*.

• See pages 22-25 for information on Mars and Jupiter

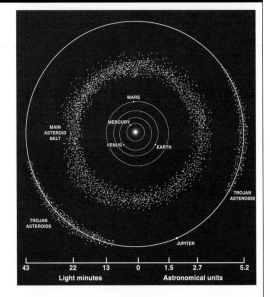

A NASA diagram showing the location of the main asteroid belt.

FIRST DISCOVERIES

A list of the first ten asteroids discovered.

Asteroid	Discovered	Size
Ceres	1801	596 miles
Pallas	1802	355 miles
Juno	1804	179 miles
Vesta	1807	326 miles
Hygeia	1849	75 miles
Eunomia	1851	127 miles
Fortuna	1852	129 miles
Psyche	1852	101 miles
Amphitrite	1854	98 miles
Euphrosyne	1854	267 miles

Ceres was discovered by the Italian astronomer Giuseppe Piazzi.

STRANGEST ASTEROIDS

- Icarus is the asteroid with the closest orbit. It comes closer to the Sun than the planet Mercury.

- The smallest asteroids are all sorts of odd shapes, because the pull of gravity is not strong enough to put them into a ball shape.

- The asteroid with the strangest shape seen so far is probably Kleopatra. It is a 137 miles long chunk of rock in the shape of a dog's bone.

ASTEROIDS WITH MOONS

- Asteroids have a very weak pull of gravity, but they are still able to attract and capture smaller asteroids as their own moons.

- An asteroid called *Ida* has a small moon, called *Dactyl*. Ida is 34.8 miles across, and its moon, Dactyl, is only about 0.62 miles across.

- An asteroid called *45 Eugenia* may have a small moon, too.

- Some asteroids travel in pairs, called *binaries*, that orbit each other.

- An asteroid called *4179 Toutatis* is thought to be two asteroids, one 1.5 miles across, and the other 0.9 miles across, that may be actually touching each other.

Nine Galileo Views in Exaggerated Color of Main-Belt Asteroid Ida

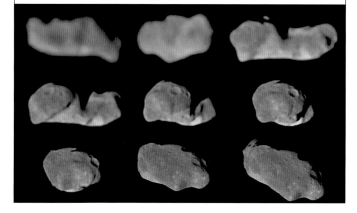

SPACE PROBES TO ASTEROIDS

A series of probes have been sent into space to learn more about asteroids.

Space probe	Details
Galileo	On its way to Jupiter, passed asteroids Gaspra in 1991 and Ida in 1993.
Hayabusa	Met with asteroid 25143 Itokawa and due to return particles from it to Earth in 2007.
NEAR-Shoemaker	Passed asteroid Mathilde on its way to 433 Eros. Orbited Eros 230 times and then landed — the first spacecraft ever to make a controlled landing on an asteroid.
Deep Space 1	Flew past asteroid 9969 Braille (formerly known as *1992KD*) on its way to a comet.

NASA montage showing encounter between *Deep Space 1* and asteroid 9969 Braille.

NEAR DISASTERS

In 1908, an asteroid slammed into Tunbuska, Siberia, flattening trees in an area 62 miles across. If this happened today, the effect would be devastation. In 1991, there was a close call when a small asteroid passed just 105,638 miles away from the Earth. Today, astronomers are looking for near-Earth objects like these. If they find them, there are various theories as to what they might be able to do to stop the threat. Some people think a nuclear missile could be launched into space to nudge the asteroid to one side.

METEORS

L ook up into a clear sky on any night and you may be lucky enough to see a streak of light. It appears for only a fraction of a second and then it is gone. The bright streak is made by a particle of dust from a meteor entering the Earth's atmosphere from space and burning up. Large meteors that travel down through the atmosphere are called *meteorioids*. When meteoroids hit the ground, they are called *meteorites*.

METEORITE FACTS

- About 500 baseball-sized rocks from space hit the ground every year.

- The largest meteorites hit the ground with such force that they make a hole called an *impact crater*.

- The biggest meteorite ever found is called the *Hoba meteorite*, after the place in Namibia where it landed. It weighs about 66 tons!

- A meteorite from Mars, called *ALH84001*, caused a stir in 1996, when some scientists thought they had found evidence of life inside it. However, most scientists now think the features seen in the meteorite are not signs of life.

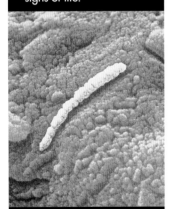

Close up of a structure found in a meteorite from Mars.

CRATERS

Large meteorites have struck Earth and left giant craters. One of the most famous of these is the Barringer Crater in Arizona (below), which measures over half a mile across. It was created 50,000 years ago by the impact of a 164-foot-wide meteorite.

METEORS

A meteor

Meteors are also called *shooting stars*, although they are not stars.

- Meteors range in size from a grain of sand to a tennis ball.

- Some meteors, called *bolides*, explode in the atmosphere with a sound like thunder.

- Meteoroids, particles from meteors, enter the Earth's atmosphere at up to about 43.5 miles per second (155,350 mph), or nearly ten times faster than the space shuttle.

- Scientists estimate that up to 4 billion meteors streak through the Earth's atmosphere every day.

METEOR SHOWERS

There are many more meteors than usual at certain times of the year. These events are called *meteor showers*.

- Meteor showers occur when the Earth flies through a trail of particles left behind by a comet.

- The Earth passes through a comet's tail in the same part of every orbit, so meteor showers occur at the same times every year.

- All the meteors in a meteor shower appear to come from the same point in the sky.

- Meteor showers are named after the constellation in whose direction the meteors appear to come.

- Some meteor showers can produce hundreds of shooting stars an hour. Meteor showers can last from a few hours to several days.

• *See pages 18–19 for information on EARTH.*

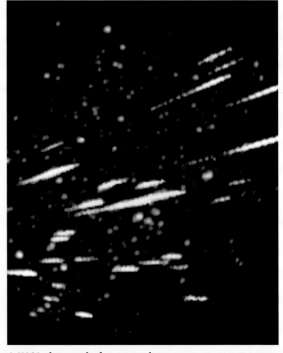

A NASA photograph of a meteor shower.

TYPES OF METEORITES

The three main types of meteorites are called *irons*, *stony meteorites*, and *stony-irons*.

- Irons are made of a mixture of iron and nickel.

- Stony-irons contain rock and iron-nickel allow.

- There are three types of stony meteorites, called *chondrites*, *carbonaceous chondrites*, and *achondrites*.

- Chondrites are made of small ball-shaped particles called *chondrules*, made of minerals that have melted and fused together.

- Chondrites may be the oldest rocks in the solar system.

- Carbonaceous chondrites contain carbon.

- Achondrites are meteorites made from stone but without the spherical chondrules found in chondrites.

- Most meteorites are chondrites.

- Achondrites may be rocks blasted out of the surface of the Moon or Mars by asteroid impacts.

stony irons

stony meteorite

iron meteorite

BEST METEOR SHOWERS

- Perseids (below) is named after the constellation *Perseus*. It can be seen between July 23 and August 22.

- Orionids is named after the constellation *Orion*. It can be seen between October 15–29.

- The meteor shower *Geminids* is named after the Gemini constellation. It can be seen in the sky between December 6–19.

THE TEN BIGGEST METEORITES

This meteorite, found in Grootfontein, Namibia, weighs nearly 66 tons.

Where	When	Weight
Hoba, Namibia	1920	66 tons
Campo del Cielo, Argentina	1969	41 tons
Cape York, Greenland	1894	34 tons
Armanty, China	1898	31 tons
Bacuberito, Mexico	1863	30 tons
Mbosi, Tanzania	1930	28 tons
Cape York, Greenland	1963	22 tons
Willamette, Oregon	1902	15 tons
Chupaderos, Mexico	1852	15 tons
Mundrabilla, Australia	1966	12 tons

PARENT COMETS

A comet whose trail produces a meteor shower is called the shower's *parent comet*.

Meteor shower	Parent comet
Eta Aquarids	Halley
Geminids	Asteroid 3200 (Phaethon)
Leonids	Tempel-Tuttle
Lyrids	Thatcher
Orionids	Halley
Perseids	Swift-Tuttle
Taurids	Encke
Ursids	Tuttle

The Eta Aquarids shower photographed in 1987.

COMETS

Every few years, an object that looks like a fuzzy star with a long, bright tail appears in the sky. These strange objects are not stars. They are comets. A comet is a chunk of dust and ice left over from the formation of the solar system. Comets orbit the Sun. When a comet nears the Sun, some of the ice on its surface evaporates and releases gas and dust to form the tail. Most comets are too dim to be seen with the naked eye, but every ten years or so an especially bright comet appears in the sky.

COMET FACTS

- About 850 comets have been spotted and listed by astronomers.

- Comets are named after their discoverers.

- Cometary nuclei (the center of comets) are usually only a few miles across.

- If all the known comets were added together, they would weigh less than the Moon.

- A comet's tail always points away from the Sun.

- The idea that a comet is made of dust and ice, like a dirty snowball, was suggested by the astronomer Fred Whipple in 1950.

- If the Earth passes through the trail of dust particles left behind by a comet, you may see lots of meteors as the dust enters the Earth's atmosphere and burns up.

The astronomer Fred Whipple in 1986.

FAMOUS COMETS

- Halley's Comet reappears every 76 years.

- It is named after the astronomer, Edmund Halley, who realized that comets seen in 1531, 1607, and 1682 were actually the same comet.

- Hale-Bopp is a long-period comet that is seen only once every few thousand years.

- Encke has the shortest period of all comets. It reappears every 3.3 years.

• See page 11
EDMUND HALLEY

THE STRUCTURE OF A COMET

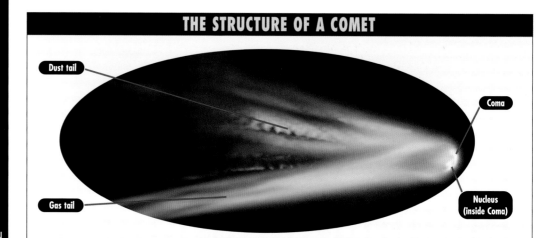

Dust tail

Coma

Nucleus (inside Coma)

Gas tail

A comet has three parts—the nucleus, the coma, and the tail.

- The nucleus is the solid part of a comet, in the middle of the comet's head.

- The coma is the gassy atmosphere that surrounds the nucleus when the comet nears the Sun.

- The tail is the long, bright stream of dust and gas that streams away from the comet.

- A comet's dust tail can be as long as 6.21 million miles long.

- The coma and tail look bright only because they reflect sunlight.

WHERE DO COMETS COME FROM?

Comets originate from two places in the solar system.

- A belt of icy objects, called the *Kuiper Belt*, begins at about the orbit of Neptune and stretches beyond the orbit of Pluto.

- A ball-shaped cloud of icy objects, called the *Oort Cloud*, surrounds the whole solar system.

- The Oort Cloud lies about 7.4 trillion miles from the Sun.

- Scientists think the Oort Cloud may contain 10 trillion comets (10 followed by 12 zeros).

- The Oort Cloud is named after the Dutch astronomer, Jan Hendrik Oort (1990–1992), who suggested the idea of the distant cloud of comets in 1950.

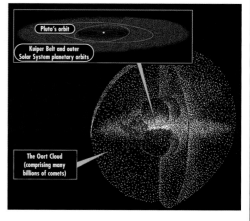

Pluto's orbit

Kuiper Belt and outer Solar System planetary orbits

The Oort Cloud (comprising many billions of comets)

A diagram (inset) showing the location of the Kuiper Belt in the solar system, and the Oort Cloud (main picture), made up of billions of comets.

• See pages 30–33 for information
on NEPTUNE and PLUTO.

COMET ORBITS

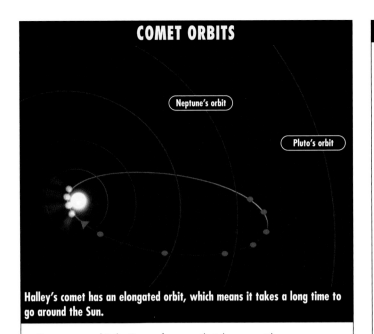

Neptune's orbit

Pluto's orbit

Halley's comet has an elongated orbit, which means it takes a long time to go around the Sun.

- Most comets orbit the Sun so far away that they cannot be seen.

- A passing planet can deflect a comet out of the Kuiper Belt and send it on a new orbit closer to the Sun.

- Oort Cloud comets are so far away that passing stars can tug them into a new orbit that takes them towards the inner solar system.

- Comets from the Kuiper Belt orbit the Sun faster than other comets. They are called *short-period comets*.

- Comets from further away in the Oort Cloud take longer to orbit the Sun. They are called *long-period comets*.

COMET HISTORY

People in the ancient world feared comets as signs of coming disasters and recorded their sightings. Even recently, sightings are greeted with a sense of wonder.

- The star that appears on the Bayeux Tapestry is thought to be Halley's Comet. The tapestry shows the Norman conquest of England in 1066.

- As recently as 1910, some people in Chicago were reported to have boarded up their windows to protect themselves from Halley's Comet.

- Records of Halley's Comet date back to 240 BC with certainty and perhaps as far back as 467 BC.

- The Great Comet of 1843 was probably the brightest comet ever seen. It was clearly visible in daylight.

Halley's comet depicted (top left) on the Bayeux Tapestry.

SOME SPACE PROBES TO COMETS

Space probe	Launched	Comet
ICE (International)	8/12/78	Flew past Giacobini-Zinner.
Vega 1 (Russia)	12/15/84	Flew past Halley.
Vega 2 (Russia)	12/21/84	Flew past Halley.
Sakigake (Japan)	1/8/85	Flew past Halley.
Giotto (Europe)	7/2/85	Flew close to Halley and photographed its nucleus.
Suisei (Japan)	8/18/85	Flew past Halley.
Stardust (USA)	2/7/99	Flew past Wild 2 and collected particles for return to Earth in 2006.
Rosetta (Europe)	3/2/04	Due to rendezvous with Churyumov-Gerasimenko in 2014.
Deep Impact (USA)	12/21/04	Flew past Tempel 1 and crashed a mini-probe into it.

Deep Impact lifts off from Launch Pad 17-B, Cape Canaveral Air Force Base.

STARS

STAR BRIGHTNESS

- How bright a star appears to be depends on how bright it really is and how far away it is.

- The closer a star is to Earth, the brighter it looks.

- Astronomers call a star's brightness its *magnitude*.

- A star's magnitude, brightness, is given by a number designation.

- The brighter a star is, the smaller or lower its magnitude is.

- Stars of magnitudes +6 or more are too faint to be seen with the naked eye.

- The Sun is the brightest object in the sky, with a magnitude of -26.8.

• See pages 12–13 for information on the SUN.

STARS TOGETHER

- Most stars are not single stars like the Sun. They have at least one companion star.

- The two stars orbit each other.

- Some pairs of stars look close together only because they lie in the same direction from Earth, but their movements show that they are not orbiting each other.

- Sometimes, two stars are so close together that one star sucks gas from the other star.

- Extra gas falling on a star may explode in a giant blast called a *nova*.

Mira A (right) with its companion star on the left.

A star is a giant ball of glowing gas in space fuelled by nuclear reactions in its core. You can see several thousand stars with the naked eye. But these are only the brightest stars. Astronomers have found tens of millions more stars by using powerful telescopes to probe the sky. Our star, the Sun, is an ordinary star. Compared to the Sun, some stars are giants. They each contain enough matter to make tens or hundreds of suns.

NAMES OF STARS

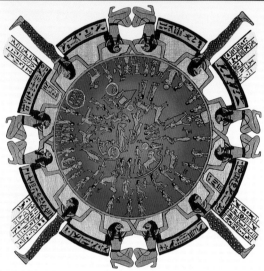

Artwork from an Egyptian temple showing the signs of the zodiac at the center.

• See pages 8–9 for information on EARLY ASTRONOMERS.

- Some of the names we know stars by today were given to them by ancient Greek and Arab astronomers perhaps two thousand years ago.

- In the 17th century, the German astronomer Johann Bayer started naming stars using Greek letters.

- The brightest star in a constellation was called *alpha*, the next brightest *beta*, and so on. For example, the brightest star in the constellation Centaurus is called *Alpha Centauri*.

- When they had used all the Greek letters, astronomers named lots of fainter stars by adding numbers to their constellation name. For example, a faint star in Pegasus is called *51 Pegasi*.

- Today, new stars are identified by numbers, often with the name of the person who discovered them and the year of discovery.

- The Hubble Space Telescope is pointed in the right direction by using a catalogue of 15 million stars whose positions are known with great accuracy.

BRIGHTEST STARS

After the Sun, the ten brightest stars seen from Earth are:

STAR	CONSTELLATION	MAGNITUDE
Sirius	Canis Major	-1.44
Canopus	Carina	-0.62
Arcturus	Bootes	-0.05
Alpha Centauri A	Centaurus	-0.01
Vega	Lyra	0.03
Capella	Auriga	0.08
Rigel	Orion	0.18
Procyon	Canis Minor	0.40
Achernar	Eridanus	0.45
Betelgeuse	Orion	0.45

The star Sirius (main picture) in the constellation Canis Major.

COLORS AND HOTNESS

Stars are different colors. The color of a star shows how hot it is.

STAR TYPE	STAR COLOR	TEMPERATURE
O	Blue	over 45,032°F
B	Blue	19,832–45,032°F
A	Blue	13,532–19,832°F
F	Blue-white	10,832–13,582°F
G	White-yellow	9,032–10,832°F
K	Orange-red	6,332–9,032°F
M	Red	below 6,332°F

CLOSEST STARS

After the Sun, the ten closest stars to Earth are:

STAR	CONSTELLATION	DISTANCE
Proxima Centauri	Centaurus	4.2 light years
Alpha Centauri	Centaurus	4.4 light years
Barnard's Star	Ophiucus	6.0 light years
Wolf 359	Leo	7.8 light years
Lalande 21185	Ursa Major	8.3 light years
Sirius	Canis Major	8.6 light years
Luyten 726-8	Cetus	8.7 light years
Ross 154	Sagittarius	9.7 light years
Ross 248	Andromeda	10.3 light years
Epsilon Eridani	Eridanus	10.5 light years

BIRTH AND DEATH OF A STAR

All stars are born from clouds of dust, and end their lives in violent explosions. They begin life as dwarfs before changing into giants or supergiants as they heat up. Depending on how much mass they start out with, they end their lives in a variety of different ways.

THE BIRTH OF A STAR

1. New stars come from giant clouds of dust and gas.

2. Knots begin to form in the gas cloud as gravity pulls it together. This compression causes the cloud to heat up.

3. Eventually, the gas begins to spiral round. Jets of gas are expelled from the poles.

4. The star's brightness increases as nucear fusion begins at its center. All the gas and dust in the space surrounding the star is blown away, and eventually the star emerges from its dusty cocoon.

5. The process is complete. The new dwarf star begins to shine.

THE DEATH OF A STAR

Whether a dwarf has changed into a giant or a supergiant will dictate how the star will eventually die.

GIANT

6. If a star uses all the hydrogen in its core, hydrogen burning will start to occur in the surrounding shells, which then become heated and cause the outer envelope of the star to swell outward.

7. As a giant's interior gets hotter and hotter, it eventually puffs away its bloated outer shell. This is called a *planetary nebula*.

8. The hot remnant left behind after a giant has passed the planetary nebula stage is called a *white dwarf*. The gravity of white dwarfs is so intense that the result is an Earth-sized remnant so dense that a small piece would weigh several tons.

DWARF

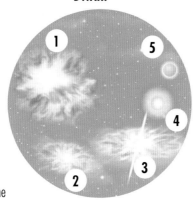

SUPERGIANT

9. Like a dwarf, a supergiant starts its life on the main sequence, but it is much hotter and brighter and can be hundreds of times the diameter of the Sun.

10. After a brilliant but short life, a supergiant dies in a spectacular explosion, called a *supernova*.

11. A supernova leaves behind an extremely dense remnant such as a neutron star or a black hole.

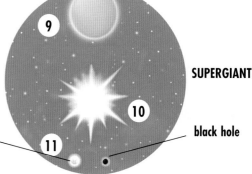

neutron star

black hole

SUPERGIANT

GIANT

Giants

A giant is a former dwarf that has cooled and expanded to a great size. In 5,000 million years from now, this will be the fate of our Sun.

Supergiants

A supergiant starts its life as a main sequence dwarf, but it is much brighter, hotter and massive than the Sun. It can be hundreds of times bigger, but it has a very short life.

- There are a total of 88 constellations.

- The ancient Egyptian astronomer, Ptolemy, listed 48 constellations in his book, the *Almagest*, written before his death in AD 150.

- European astronomers added another 40 constellations in the 17th and 18th centuries.

- During the early 1900s, the International Astronomical Union mapped the boundaries between. Every star now belongs to a constellation.

• See pages 8–9 for information on EARLY ASTRONOMERS.

FINDING NAMES

- Most constellations were named according to religious beliefs and mythological characters.

- The oldest constellations were probably named more than 4,000 years ago.

- The ancient Greeks had no names for constellations in these southernmost skies, because the stars were not visible from Greece.

- European astronomers filled in the gaps between the northern constellations and began naming the southern constellations.

- The final gaps in the southern constellations were filled by the French astronomer, Nicolas Louis de Lacaille.

STAR CONSTELLATIONS

People have seen patterns in the stars for thousands of years. The groups of stars that form these patterns are called *constellations*. The stars in a constellation rarely have any connection with each other. They simply lie in the same direction when viewed from Earth. Twelve of the most ancient constellations have special significance. They are the twelve constellations the Sun, Moon and brightest planets pass through. They are also known as the *signs of the zodiac*. The ancient constellations are still used by astronomers as guides to find their way around the night sky.

Winter sky

Orion, the Hunter is a magnificent constellation visible during late evenings in winter. The three stars in its belt can be used as a celestial guide. Just below the belt is a shiny patch called the *Orion Nebula*, which is a splendid sight through binoculars or a small telescope. The Orion Nebula is a stellar "nursery," where stars are being born right now.

GEMINI

A slightly curving line drawn upward through Rigel and Betelgeuse will get you to Gemini, with its two bright stars Castor and Pollux, the *Heavenly Twins*.

AURIGA

Over Orion's head is Auriga, the Charioteer. Near the bright star Capella is a distinctive triangle of stars called the *Kids*.

PERSEUS

Now follow a line northeast of Orion past Taurus to Perseus. This constellation contains a double open cluster.

CANIS MINOR

A line to the west of Orion takes you to the small constellation Canis Minor, the Little Dog. The three stars Procyon (in Canis Minor), Betelgeuse (in Orion), and Sirius (in Canis Major) form the prominent Winter Triangle.

TAURUS

Follow the three stars of Orion's belt upward to the constellation Taurus, the Bull. Taurus contains the bright red star Aldebaran. This star appears to form part of the "v" of the Hyades, an open star cluster. In fact, Aldebaran is a foreground star and is not part of this distant group. Continuing the line from Orion's belt further, there is a close-knit bunch of stars called *Pleiades*. These stars form yet another open cluster.

CANIS MAJOR

Canis Major, the Big Dog, is found by following Orion's belt downward. It contains Sirius, the brightest star in the sky.

LEPUS

Beneath Orion is a constellation called *Lepus*, the Hare.

ERIDANUS

Eridanus, the River, is a faint constellation that manages to travel a sixth of the way around the sky. It lies to the right of Orion, just past Rigel.

ORION

- Orion is one of the oldest constellations.

- More than a thousand years ago, it was known as *Tammuz* to the Chaldeans.

- Tammuz was the name of the month when the three stars across its middle rose before sunrise.

- The Syrians knew it as *Al Jabbar* (The Giant).

- The ancient Egyptians knew it as *Sahu*, the soul of the god Osiris.

- The name we know it by is *Orion*.

- In Greek mythology, Orion was a giant hunter.

Orion's Belt

Spring sky

When you look up at the late evening sky in spring, you should be able to see the seven stars of the Big Dipper. Use the Big Dipper (marked below in red) to navigate around the sky.

CEPHEUS

A straight line through Merak and Dubhe in the Big Dipper and Polaris is Cepheus, a dim constellation.

DRACO

Between Ursa Major and Ursa Minor is long, winding Draco, the Dragon, a fairly dim constellation.

BOOTES

The three left-hand stars of the Big Dipper can be used to trace a gentle curve downward to the bright orange star Arcturus in the constellation *Bootes*, the Herdsman.

LEO

Directly below the Big Dipper is the constellation *Leo*, the Lion. It is one of the few constellations that bears even the slightest resemblance to its name. Its bright star, Regulus, is the dot in an backckward question mark of stars known as the *Sickle*.

CASSIOPEIA

A line from Mizar in the Big Dipper through Polaris is the constellation *Cassiopeia*, a "w"-shaped constellation through which parts of the Milky Way pass.

URSA MINOR

Follow the two stars Merak and Dubhe in the Big Dipper north to Polaris, the Pole Star, in the constellation *Ursa Minor*, the Little Bear.

URSA MAJOR & THE BIG DIPPER

The Big Dipper is not actually a constellation, but the brightest part of the constellation Ursa Major, the Big Bear. The most important thing about the Big Dipper is that some of its stars make useful guides to other parts of the sky.

(Star chart labels: CASSIOPEIA, CEPHEUS, DRACO, Polaris, URSA MINOR, Dubhe, Mizar, Merak, URSA MAJOR, BOOTES, Arcturus, LEO, Regulus)

TELESCOPES

Astronomers have used telescopes to study the sky for about 400 years. The first telescopes magnified images of distant objects using lenses. A new type of telescope had curved mirrors instead of lenses, which allows better magnification. Astronomers use telescopes to collect all sorts of waves and rays, including visible light from space to learn more about stars, galaxies, and other objects.

TYPES OF LIGHT

Light is a form of radiation that moves in waves. Each of the colors of the rainbow has its own wavelength. The entire range of wavelengths is called the *electromagnetic spectrum*. The Earth's atmosphere blocks many of the wavelengths, but from space, the entire spectrum is visible. By studying what kindof radiation is emitted from objects such as stars, astronomers can learn about an object's density, temperature, chemical composition, and how it moves.

visible light

← radio waves → infrared ← X-ray →

microwaves | ultra violet | gamma rays

← wavelength increases

TELESCOPE PARTS

- A refracting telescope, or refractor, collects light with a large objective lens. The image is viewed through a smaller eyepiece lens.

- A reflecting telescope collects light with a large primary, or main, mirror and reflects it to an eyepiece, cameras, or other instruments through a smaller secondary mirror.

- Large mirrors sag under their own weight, so the biggest reflecting telescopes have mirrors made in smaller sections joined together.

- Each of the two Keck telescopes on Mauna Kea, Hawaii, has a 32 foot primary mirror made from 36 segments.

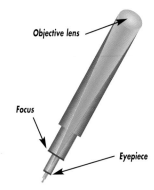

Objective lens

Focus

Eyepiece

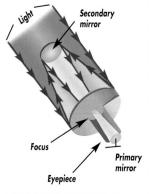

Light

Secondary mirror

Focus

Primary mirror

Eyepiece

REFRACTING TELESCOPE

1. The objective lens catches the light and brings it to a focus.

2. The eyepiece magnifies the focused image.

REFLECTING TELESCOPE

1. Light falls through the top of the open-frame tube, and heads towards the primary mirror.

2. It is then reflected up the tube to the smaller, secondary mirror.

3. The light is then reflected back down the tube, through a hole in the primary, to the focus (located beneath the primary).

TYPES OF TELESCOPE

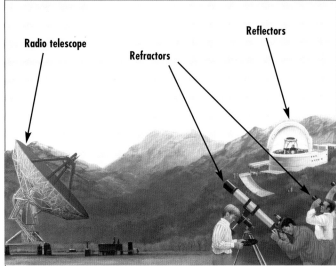

Radio telescope

Refractors

Reflectors

Telescopes can be classified in different ways. They can be divided according to the way they produce a magnified image.

- Refractors use lenses to form an image.

- Reflectors use curved mirrors to form an image.

- Refractors and reflectors collect and magnify light, but telescopes can make use of other types of energy.

- Radio telescopes use radio waves, infrared telescopes use infrared rays, X-ray telescopes use X-rays, ultraviolet telescopes use UV waves, and gamma ray telescopes use gamma rays.

• See pages 10–11 LATER ASTRONOMERS

MAKING SHARP IMAGES

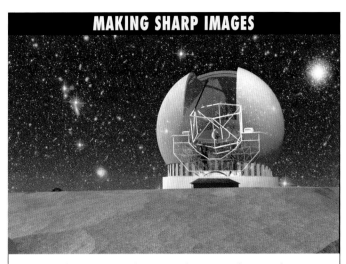

The California Extremely Large Telescope in the United States.

- Starlight is distorted as it travels down through the Earth's atmosphere to the ground.

- The distorting effect of the atmosphere makes stars appear to twinkle, and also makes it difficult for astronomers to take clear photographs of them.

- Astronomers avoid the distorting effect of the atmosphere by placing their telescopes on top of mountains, above the thickest part of the atmosphere.

- Telescopes in space, above the atmosphere, have the clearest view of all.

- Some reflecting telescopes have adaptive optics. The mirror continually changes shape to cancel the effect of the atmosphere and produce sharper images.

- Some telescopes work only in space because the energy they use to make images is blocked by the Earth's atmosphere.

SPACE TELESCOPES

TELESCOPE	LAUNCHED	USED TO STUDY
Beppo-Sax	1996	X-rays
Chandra X-ray Observatory	1999	X-rays
Compton Gamma Ray Observatory	1991	gamma rays
Einstein (HEAO-2)	1978	X-rays
Hipparcos	1989	star positions
Hubble Space Telescope	1990	stars, galaxies, nebulae
Infra-red Astronomical telescope	1983	infrared waves
International Space Observatory	1995	infrared waves
International Ultraviolet Explorer	1978	ultraviolet waves
Solar and Heliospheric Observatory	1995	the Sun
Spitzer Space Telescope	2003	infrared waves
Uhuru	1970	X-rays

LINKING TELESCOPES

The amount of detail a telescope can see depends on how much light or other energy it collects.

- When several telescopes are pointed in the same direction and linked together, they behave like a larger telescope.

- The twin Keck telescopes in Hawaii have mirrors 33 feet across, but when they are linked together, they behave like one telescope with a mirror 279 feet across.

- The European Very Large Telescope (VLT) has four mirrors, each 27 feet across. When linked together, they are like a telescope with a 656-foot mirror.

TELESCOPES OF THE FUTURE

- The Giant Magellan Telescope will be nearly 72 feet across and it will have seven huge 27-foot mirrors.

- The Thirty Meter Telescope, with a mirror 98 feet across (30 meters), will be in Hawaii, Chile, or Mexico.

- The European large Telescope (ELT) will have a mirror 328 feet across, about ten times the size of the biggest telescope mirrors today.

- In 2007, the Herschel Space Observatory will be launched to study infrared and extremely small waves.

- The Hubble Space Telescope's successor, the James Webb Space Telescope, will be launched around 2013.

TELESCOPE TIMELINE

1610
Galileo Galilei becomes the first person to study the night sky through a telescope.

1668
Sir Isaac Newton builds the first reflecting telescope.

1845
Lord Rosse builds a giant 72-inch telescope at Birr Castle in Parsonstown, Irleand.

1895
The Yerkes 40-inch refractor is built in Williams Bay, Wisconsin.

1908
The Mount Wilson 100-inch reflecting telescope begins operation in California.

1937
Karl Jansky builds the first radio telescope.

1937
Grote Reber builds a 31-foot radio telescope.

1957
The 250-foot Jodrell Bank steerable radio telescope is completed.

1963
The 1,000-foot Arecibo radio telescope in Puerto Rico begins operating.

1974
The 153-inch Anglo-Australian telescope in Australia opens.

1979
The 150-inch UKIRT, 140-inch optical reflector and NASA Infrared Facility begin work on Mauna Kea, Hawaii.

1990
The Hubble Space Telescope is launched by the space shuttle.

1993
The first 33-foot Keck telescope begins operating at Mauna Kea, Hawaii.

1996
Keck II begins operating on Mauna Kea, Hawaii.

2003
The Spitzer Space Telescope is launched in August.

MILKY WAY

O ur star, the Sun, is one of billions of stars that travel through space together. This vast collection of stars is the Milky Way galaxy. On a clear dark night, you may be able to see the hazy band of the Milky Way stretching across the sky. The stars are held together by the pull of their gravity.

GALAXY PROFILE

Shape	**Spiral**
Diameter of disc	**100,000 light years**
Average thickness of disc	**10,000 light years**
Diameter of central bulge	**12,000 light years**
Thickness of central bulge	**30,000 light years**
Number of stars	**200-400 billion**

An artist's impression of the Milky Way.

AGE OF THE MILKY WAY

- Astronomers think the Milky Way formed soon after the universe began.

- The Milky Way probably formed when the universe was only about 200-300 million years old.

- This means the age of the Milky Way is about 13,000–13,600 million years old.

Globular cluster NGC 6397 contains some of the oldest stars in the Milky Way.

MILKY WAY CENTER

- We cannot see the center of the Milky Way because it is surrounded by thick clouds of gas and dust.

- Astronomers think there may be a giant black hole at the center, possibily containing as much matter as a million Suns.

- Earth is in no danger of falling into the Milky Way's black hole.

- The Sun is located about two-thirds of the way out from the center of the Milky Way, toward its edge.

- The center is about 25,000 light years away from us.

An artist's impression of the Milky Way.

• See pages 48–49 for information on GALAXIES.

MANY ARMS

The Milky Way has four main spiral arms that curl out from the center of the galaxy. These are the Norma Arm, the Scutum-Crux Arm, the Sagittarius Arm, and the Perseus Arm. The Sun lies in a small arm called the *Orion Arm*, also called the *Local Arm*.

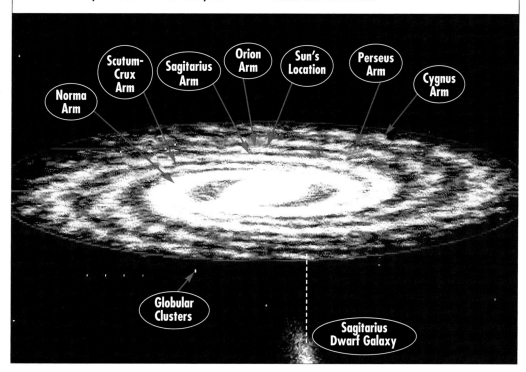

- Norma Arm
- Scutum-Crux Arm
- Sagitarius Arm
- Orion Arm
- Sun's Location
- Perseus Arm
- Cygnus Arm
- Globular Clusters
- Sagitarius Dwarf Galaxy

IN A SPIN

Sun's path around the Galaxy

- The Milky Way slowly spins as it moves through space like a giant cartwheel.

- The Sun takes about 226 million years to complete one orbit.

- The Sun moves around the Milky Way at a speed of 136.7 miles per second.

- The Sun has orbited the center of the Milky Way about 25 times since its formation.

• See pages 12–13 for information on the SUN.

SPEEDING STARS

The majority of the stars in the Sun's vicinity in the Milky Way move around the galaxy around 18–31 miles per second. There are, however, some stars that travel around twice as fast as that.

NEAREST GALAXIES

GALAXY	DISTANCE FROM EARTH
Canis Major Dwarf Galaxy	25,000 light years
Sagittarius Dwarf Elliptical Galaxy	81,000 light years
Large Magellanic Cloud	160,000 light years
Small Magellanic Cloud	190,000 light years
Ursa Minor Dwarf Galaxy	205,500 light years

The Sagittarius Dwarf Elliptical Galaxy.

FUTURE FATE

The Milky Way is slowly moving towards another galaxy called the *Andromeda galaxy*.

- Andromeda is bigger than the Milky Way.

- One day, the two galaxies will collide, but they will not meet for several billion years.

- The two galaxies will probably merge and form a new galaxy.

- The new galaxy will not be a spiral like the Milky Way, but it will probably be elliptical in shape.

- The Milky Way has already swallowed up many small nearby galaxies.

The two illustrations below simulate what might happen when the Andromeda galaxy hits ours. The central regions will merge into a single galaxy.

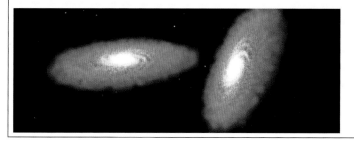

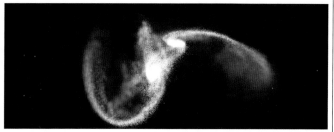

GALAXIES

• See page 11
EDWIN HUBBLE

There are billions of giant star groups like the Milky Way. They are called *galaxies*. Some galaxies are spiral in shape like the Milky Way. Others are different shapes. Galaxies are not spread evenly through space. They bunch together in groups, called *clusters*. The clusters bunch together in bigger groups, called *superclusters*. Our galaxy, the Milky Way, belongs to a cluster of about 30 galaxies, called the *Local Group*. This is one of about 400 clusters of galaxies that form the *Local Supercluster*.

GALAXY NAMES

- Galaxies known for a long time were named after their discoverer.

- The Large Magellanic Cloud is named after the explorer, Ferdinand Magellan, whose crew discovered it during the first voyage around the world in the 1520s.

- Some galaxies are named after the constellation they are in.

- The Sagittarius galaxy is named after the Sagittarius constellation that it appears in.

- Today, galaxies are named differently. They are usually known by the name of a catalog they are listed in and their number in the catalog.

- The New Galactic Catalog (NGC) lists hundreds of galaxies. They all have an NGC number.

- Some galaxies are also known by an "M" number. They are galaxies that appear in a list written in 1781 by the French astronomer Charles Messier. In this list, the Andromeda galaxy is M31.

- Some galaxies appear in more than one list and so they have more than one name or number. For example, NGC 598 is also known as M33.

GALAXY SHAPES

Irregular

Elliptical

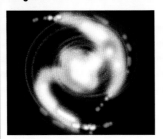

Barred Spiral

Spiral

All galaxies have one of three basic shapes: spiral, elliptical, or irregular.

- Nearly all galaxies are either spiral or elliptical.

- Elliptical galaxies may be perfectly ball-shaped or they may be flattened, stretched oval shapes.

- Spiral galaxies usually have a central bulge of older stars surrounded by a disc of matter where new stars are forming.

- Stars in a spiral galaxy's disc trace out the shapes of spiral arms.

- About half of all spiral galaxies have a straight bar of stars through the central bulge.

- These galaxies are called *barred spirals*.

- Irregular galaxies have no definite shape.

- Some irregular galaxies look as if they were once spirals. They may have changed shape when they collided with other galaxies.

- Other irregular galaxies are groups of stars.

- This way of dividing galaxies into groups according to their shape was devised by the astronomer Edwin Hubble in the 1920s.

ACTIVE GALAXIES

Active galaxies give out far more light and other energy than their stars should produce.

- In the 1960s, astronomers discovered objects that looked like stars, but they were distant galaxies with a brilliant core 100 times brighter than a normal galaxy.

- These active galaxies are called *quasi-stellar objects*, or *quasars*.

- The blindingly bright core of a quasar is only about the size of our solar system, but brighter than many Milky Way galaxies.

- The huge amount of light pouring out of a quasar seems to be coming from matter falling into a black hole.

- The black hole at the center of a quasar is massive, perhaps a billion times the mass of the Sun.

The Chandra X-Ray observatory (model shown here) will allow researchers to obtain better X-ray images of quasars.

HOW GALAXIES MOVE

Astronomers can tell a lot about a distant galaxy by studying the light and other energy that it gives out.

- A galaxy gives out known patterns of light according to the chemical elements it contains.

- When astronomers analyze light from distant galaxies, these distinctive patterns look wrong. The colors seem to have been shifted toward the red end of the spectrum of visible light.

This is called *red shift*.

- Red shift happens because the light waves have been stretched. Stretching light waves changes the colors they make.

- Light waves are stretched like this when they come from something that is rushing away from us.

- This indicates that all the galaxies we can see are flying away from us.

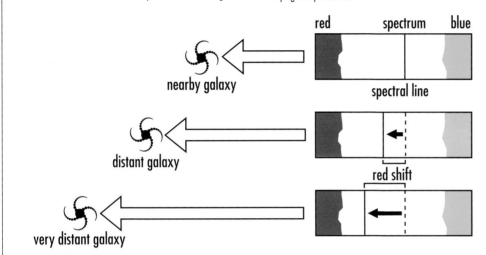

nearby galaxy

distant galaxy

very distant galaxy

red   spectrum   blue

spectral line

red shift

HOW MANY GALAXIES?

- No one knows the exact number of galaxies that exist today.

- Astronomers see galaxies wherever they look in the sky.

- When they pointed their most powerful telescopes and most sensitive cameras at a tiny part of the sky only one tenth the diameter of the Moon that seemed to be empty, they found 10,000 galaxies there.

- There are certainly billions of galaxies.

• See pages 44–45 for information on TELESCOPES.

FARTHEST GALAXIES

- The furthest galaxies observed so far are about 13 billion light years away from us.

- These galaxies are so far away that light from them has travelled across the universe for 13 billion years to reach us.

- Astronomers are seeing these distant galaxies as they looked 13 billion years ago when the light left them.

- This was only just after the universe formed, so even if there are farther galaxies, light from them would not have time to reach us. These distant galaxies may not be there any more. Even if they still exist, they probably look very different today.

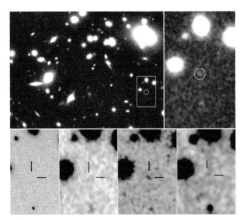

European Southern observatory image of Abell 1835 IR1916, the most distant galaxy yet discovered, located about 13,230 million light years away.

LARGEST LOCAL GALAXIES

Galaxy	Type	Diameter	Distance
Andromeda	Spiral	130,000 light years	2.5 million light years
Milky Way	Spiral	100,000 light years	-
NGC 598	Spiral	60,000 light years	2.7 million light years
Large Magellanic Cloud	Irregular	30,000 light years	160,000 light years
Small Magellanic Cloud	Irregular	25,000 light years	180,000 light years

Andromeda

49

THE UNIVERSE

- Scientists believe that there is a lot more matter in the universe than we can see.

- Most of the matter in the universe is invisible, but scientists can detect the effect of its gravity, which is how we know it exists.

- This invisible matter is called *dark matter*.

- No one yet knows what dark matter is made of.

The universe is all the matter, energy, space and time that exists everywhere. Scientists have many theories to explain how and when the universe began. Today, most scientists agree that the universe burst into existence about 13.7 billion years ago in a huge explosion called the *Big Bang*. It flung matter and energy in all directions and produced the universe we see today.

EXPANSION OF THE UNIVERSE

The galaxies all appear to be moving away from us at very great speeds.

This is not because we occupy any special position in the universe, exactly the same thing would be observed from any other galaxy. In fact, it is not the galaxies that are moving, but the space between them that is expanding. Imagine sticking stars on a balloon and then blowing the balloon up. The stars would seem to move apart as the balloon inflates.The expansion of the universeis a process that has been occurring over billions of years.

COSMOLOGY

- The branch of science concerned with studying the origin and development of the universe is called *cosmology*.

- Scientists who study cosmology are called *cosmologists*.

- Cosmologists may never look through telescopes. They often rely on information about stars, galaxies, and other objects from the people who actually observe them, caled *astronomers*.

Cosmologist Albert Einstein

• See pages 8–11 for information on ASTRONOMERS.

NEW THEORIES

Scientists are still developing new theories to explain the origin and evolution of the universe.

- According to string theory, particles of matter are actually tiny vibrating loops and strands of energy.

- The strings may lie on sheets or tubes of space, called *membranes*, or *branes*.

- String theory predicts that there are another six dimensions, as well as the three dimensions in space and one in time that we already know about.

- Another prediction of string theory is that there may be many more universes as well as ours.

- These parallel universes are called a *multiverse*.

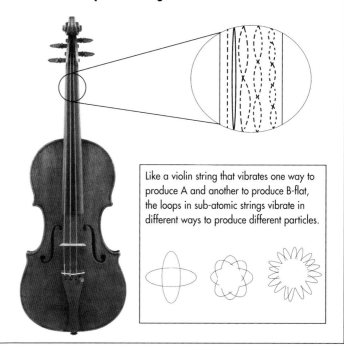

Like a violin string that vibrates one way to produce A and another to produce B-flat, the loops in sub-atomic strings vibrate in different ways to produce different particles.

THE BIG BANG

Most scientists think the universe began from a tiny speck that exploded at the start of space and time, called the *Big Bang*.

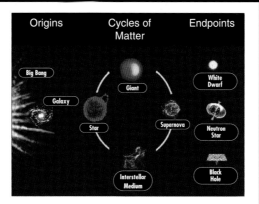

- In its first moment of existence, the universe was unimaginably hot.

- It expanded rapidly, a stage called *inflation*.

- As the universe expanded, it cooled.

- Within a fraction of a second, the first particles were produced.

- One second after the Big Bang, the temperature had fallen to 10 billion degrees.

- After three minutes, the temperature was one billion degrees — cool enough for particles of matter to join together.

- About 300,000 years after the explosion, it was cool enough for whole atoms to form.

- Hydrogen, helium ,and other simple elements formed.

- Matter was not spread evenly through the early universe.

- Denser clumps of matter developed into the first stars and galaxies only about 200 million years after the Big Bang.

- The Big Bang produced an expanding universe, which we see today.

- The Big Bang also led to the creation of hydrogen and helium in the proportions we see today.

- In the 1950s, scientists suggested that if the Big Bang really happened, its echo should still exist.

- As the universe expanded, the super-hot radiation that filled it spread out and cooled.

- Today, this radiation still exists.

- It is called the *cosmic background radiation* or *cosmic microwave background*.

- Two astronomers, Arno Penzias and Robert Wilson, detected the Cosmic Background Radiation in 1965.

- In 1995, the Cosmic Background Explorer (COBE) satellite made a map of the background radiation.

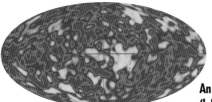

An image of the universe taken by the COBE satellite (left) confirming a temperature of temperature of -454°F.

COSMOLOGIST TIMELINE

Ptolemy (AD 87–150)
His book *Almagest* stated Earth is at the center of the universe.

Nicolaus Copernicus (1473–1543)
Proposed that the Sun is at the center of the universe.

Tycho Brahe (1546–1601)
Said that the stars are not carried around on crystal spheres, but fly through the sky unsupported.

Galileo Galilei (1564–1642)
Made observations showing that Copernicus was right.

Sir Isaac Newton (1642–1727)
Developed the theory of gravity that extended far beyond Earth to the Moon and space.

Friedrich Bessel (1784–1846)
Measured the distances to some of the closest stars.

William Parsons (1800–1867)
Made the first detailed observations of spiral galaxies.

Albert Einstein (1879–1955)
Showed the relationships between space and time and between matter and energy.

Harlow Shapley (1885–1972)
Calculated the size of the Milky Way galaxy and found the location of the Sun within it.

Edwin Hubble (1889–1953)
Discovered that other galaxies are outside the Milky Way and that the universe expands uniformly.

THE FUTURE OF THE UNIVERSE

What will be the eventual fate of the universe? Everything depends on how dense the universe is. There are three possibilities;

- If the density is higher than a certain value, called the *critical density*, then the universe will eventually stop expanding and collapse on itself. This is called the *Big Crunch Scenario*.

- If the density is less than critical, then the universe will continue expanding, and the temperature of everything in the universe will plummet. This scenario is called the *Heat Death Scenario*.

- Finally, if the density is just borderline, the universe will expand less and less, but will not collapse. This is called the *Flat Universe Scenario*.

A balloon experiment, called *Boomerang*, was sent high into the atmosphere above the Antarctic, to measure the "bumpiness" in the cosmic background. This measurement shows that the universe is actually flat.

The balloon experiment *Boomerang* with a projection of its results superimposed behind.

GEMINI (USA)

Gemini 4 astronaut Ed White during his spacewalk over El Paso, Texas.

- *Gemini* was a two-person spacecraft, launched by the *Titan* rocket. There were ten manned Gemini spaceflights in 1965 and 1966.

- Ed White made the first spacewalk by an American astronaut during the *Gemini 4* mission.

- *Gemini* allowed astronauts to practice all the maneuvers that would be needed for a moon-landing mission.

- The longest *Gemini* mission was *Gemini 7*, which lasted for 13 days and 18 hours.

HUMAN BEINGS IN SPACE

Human beings have been traveling into space since 1961. The first manned spacecraft were just big enough to fit one person inside. Later, spacecraft could fly three people around the world or take them all the way to the Moon and back. At first, these spacecraft were used for only one space mission each. The US space shuttle is different. It can be flown again and again. Until 2003, Russia and the USA were the only countries with a manned space program, but in that year, China launched its first manned space mission. *Shenzhou-5* carried Yang Liwei into space on October 15. He returned home safely after orbiting Earth 14 times.

VOSTOK (USSR/RUSSIA)

Vostok was the first manned spacecraft and the culmination of a space race between the United States and the Soviet Union.

- The *Vostok* capsule was a small sphere only 8.2 feet across.

- The Soviet Union called its space travellers *cosmonauts*.

- Each capsule carried one cosmonaut into space for missions lasting up to five days.

- The first cosmonaut was Yuri Gagarin.

- He made the first ever manned spaceflight on April 12, 1961.

- On the way back, Gagarin was ejected from his capsule at a height of 2,966 feet and landed by parachute.

- The first manned spaceflight lasted less than two hours from launch to landing.

- *Vostok 6* launched Valentina Tereshkova, the first woman in space, on June 16, 1963.

The *Vostok 1* space capsule.

The cosmonaut Yuri Gagarin.

MERCURY (USA)

The US answered *Vostok* with its own one-person space capsule, called *Mercury*.

- After re-entry, *Mercury* capsules landed in the sea.

- America's first astronaut was Alan Shepard. He made a 15-minute sub-orbital flight (into space, but not around the Earth) in *Mercury 3* on May 5, 1961.

- Alan Shepard was the only *Mercury* astronaut who would later walk on the Moon.

- Virgil Grissom's *Mercury 4* capsule sank soon after it splashed down. Grissom was rescued.

- *Mercury 6* carried the first American to go into orbit, John Glenn, on February 20, 1962.

- There was an emergency during Glenn's flight when ground controllers thought his spacecraft's heat shield had come loose, but he landed safely.

- There were six manned *Mercury* missions between 1961 and 1963.

The recovered *Mercury* space capsule.

APOLLO (USA)

The *Apollo* spacecraft were designed to take three astronauts to the Moon's orbit and land two of them on the Moon.

- The *Apollo* spacecraft were made of three modules — the Command Module, the Service Module, and the Lunar Excursion Module (LEM).

- The crew spent most of their time in the Command Module, supplied with air, electricity and rocket power by the Service Module.

- The LEM was the part of the spacecraft that landed on the Moon.

- The tiny Command Module was the only part of the spacecraft to return to Earth and splash down in the Pacific Ocean.

- The spacecraft was launched by the giant *Saturn V* rocket.

- The crew of Apollo 8 were the first humans to orbit the Moon.

- After four manned test-flights, *Apollo 11* landed Neil Armstrong and Buzz Aldrin on the Moon's surface in 1969, while Michael Collins circled the Moon.

- The *Apollo 13* spacecraft suffered a serious explosion on its way to the Moon. The crew returned to Earth safely.

- The *Apollo 13* crew travelled further from Earth than anyone else — 248,666 miles.

- The last three *Apollo* missions carried an electric car called the *Lunar Rover*, which astronauts used to travel further on the Moon.

- The last *Apollo* Moon-landing mission was *Apollo 17* in 1972. The *Apollo 17* crew stayed on the Moon for the longest time — 75 hours.

- Over six missions, 12 *Apollo* astronauts landed on the Moon and brought moon rocks back to Earth. They also left packages of scientific instruments on the Moon's surface.

- Leftover *Apollo* hardware was used for a joint US-Soviet mission called the *Apollo-Soyuz Test Project* and also for the *Skylab* space station.

• See pages 20–21 for information on the MOON.

SOYUZ (USSR/RUSSIA)

***Soyuz* was initially designed as part of the USSR's Moon mission, and it is the longest serving manned spacecraft in the world.**

- A *Soyuz* spacecraft has three modules — an instrument module, a re-entry module, and an orbital module. The spacecraft is 22.97 feet long and 8.86 feet in diameter.

- The re-entry module lands by parachute on the ground. It fires rockets just before touching the ground to cushion the impact.

- The first manned *Soyuz* mission took place in 1967. Unfortunately, the spacecraft crashed and killed the crew of one, Vladimir Komarov. Since then, *Soyuz* has been a highly successful and reliable spacecraft.

- *Soyuz* spacecraft ferry cosmonauts and astronauts to and from the new *International Space Station*.

- A type of unmanned *Soyuz* spacecraft, called *Progress*, was developed to deliver supplies to space stations.

SPACE SHUTTLE (USA)

The development of a reusable space vehicle was the next stage in man's exploration of space.

- The space shuttle orbiter is the size of a small airliner. It is 121 feet long with a wingspan of 79 feet.

- The payload bay carries satellites, laboratories, and scientific instruments into space.

- The space shuttle has a crew of two pilots and up to five other astronauts.

- It is launched with the help of two rocket boosters and an external fuel tank, which supplies fuel to the three big engines in the orbiter's tail.

- The first space shuttle was launched into space for the first time in 1981, crewed by John Young and Bob Crippen.

- Since 1981, there have been more than 100 space shuttle missions.

- The oldest shuttle astronaut was John Glenn, at the age of 77 years. He is the same John Glenn who made the first US orbital flight in 1962.

- There are currently three shuttles, called *Discovery*, *Atlantis*, and *Endeavour*.

- Two other shuttles, *Columbia* and *Challenger*, were lost along with their crews in accidents.

SPACE PROBES

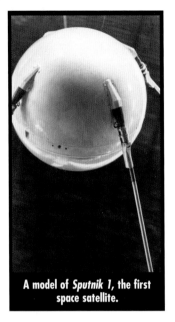

A model of *Sputnik 1*, the first space satellite.

uman beings have traveled only as far as the Moon, but unmanned space probes have traveled almost the entire solar system. The first probes were blasted into space toward the end of the 1950s when the Cold War between the United States and the USSR was at its height. They have explored the surface of Mars, created maps of Venus, taken close-up photographs of nearly all the planets and many of their moons, orbited Saturn and even left the solar system altogether. There are too many space probes to list them all, but details of a few of the most important probes are given here.

SPUTNIK (USSR/RUSSIA)

PROBE	LAUNCHED	DETAILS
Sputnik 1	Oct. 4, 1957	The world's first artificial satellite
Sputnik 2	Nov. 3, 1957	Carried dog Laika, the first living space traveller
Sputnik 3	May 15, 1958	Attempted to study solar radiation
Sputnik 4	May 15, 1960	Unmanned test-flight for *Vostok 1*
Sputnik 5	Aug. 19, 1960	Carried two dogs, Belka and Strelka
Sputnik 6	Dec. 1, 1960	The second test-flight for *Vostok*. Recovery failed
Sputnik 7	Feb. 4, 1961	A test-flight for Venus probe *Sputnik 8*
Sputnik 8	Feb. 12, 1961	Launched Russia's first Venus probe
Sputnik 9	Mar. 9, 1961	Carried the dog Chernushka
Sputnik 10	Mar. 25, 1961	Carried the dog Zvezdochka

Laika, the first animal in space.

PIONEER (USA)

PROBE	LAUNCHED	DETAILS
Pioneer 1	Oct. 11, 1958	Mapped the Van Allen radiation belts around Earth
Pioneer 2	Nov. 8, 1958	Intended to reach the Moon, but failed
Pioneer 3	Dec. 6, 1958	Failed to reach the Moon
Pioneer 4	Mar. 3, 1959	Passed within 37,282 miles of the Moon
Pioneer 5	Mar. 11, 1960	Entered solar orbit, sent solar flare and solar wind data
Pioneer 6	Dec. 16, 1965	Entered solar orbit and studied the Sun's atmosphere
Pioneer 7	Aug. 17 1966	Combined with *Pioneer 6* to study the Sun
Pioneer 8	Dec. 13, 1967	Joined *Pioneer 6* and *7* to study the Sun
Pioneer 9	Nov. 8, 1968	Joined *Pioneer 6*, *7*, and *8* to study the Sun
Pioneer 10	Mar. 3, 1972	Passed within about 80,778 miles of Jupiter's cloud-tops
Pioneer 11	Apr. 5, 1973	Photographed Jupiter's south pole
Pioneer Venus Orbiter	May 20, 1978	Orbited Venus, studied atmosphere
Pioneer Venus Multiprobe	Aug. 8, 1978	Dropped four probes into Venus's atmosphere before entering the atmosphere and burning up

The *Pioneer Venus Orbiter*, launched in May 1978.

VENUS PROBES (USSR/RUSSIA)

PROBE	LAUNCHED	DETAILS
Venera 1	Feb. 12, 1961	First interplanetary flight passed within 62,137 miles of Venus
Venera 2	Nov. 12, 1965	Passed within 14,912 miles of Venus
Venera 3	Nov. 16, 1965	First spacecraft to land on another planet
Venera 4	June 12, 1967	Transmitted data during descent through atmosphere
Venera 5	Jan. 5, 1969	Transmitted data during descent through atmosphere
Venera 6	Jan. 10, 1969	Transmitted data during descent through atmosphere
Venera 7	Aug. 17, 1970	Transmitted data from the surface of Venus
Venera 8	Mar. 27, 1972	Transmitted data from the surface of Venus
Venera 9	June 8, 1975	First spacecraft to send pictures from the surface of another planet
Venera 10	June 14, 1975	Transmitted pictures from the surface of Venus
Venera 11	Sept. 9, 1978	Flyby probe dropped a lander onto Venus
Venera 12	Sept. 14, 1978	Flyby probe dropped a lander onto Venus
Venera 13	Oct. 30, 1981	Landed using radar maps made by *Pioneer-Venus* probe
Venera 14	Nov. 4, 1981	Flyby probe dropped a lander onto Venus
Venera 15	June 2, 1983	Orbited Venus and mapped surface by radar
Venera 16	June 6, 1983	Orbited Venus and mapped its surface by radar

Venera 13 replica at the Cosmos Pavillion in Moscow.

• See pages 16–17 for information on VENUS.

VIKINGS TO MARS (US)

In 1976, the US landed two *Viking* spacecraft on the red planet.

PROBE	LAUNCHED
Viking 1	August 20, 1975
Viking 2	September 9, 1975

- After the US *Mariner* Mars probes in the 1960s and 1970s had revealed Mars to be a cratered Moon-like world, scientists wantedn to land a spacecraft on the surface.
- Both of the *Viking* missions placed an orbiter in orbit around Mars, while a lander descended to the surface.
- The landers tested the Martian soil and atmosphere and sent data back to Earth via the orbiters.
- They found no definite signs of life.
- The *Viking* probes also took the first high-quality close-up color photographs of the Martian surface (see below).

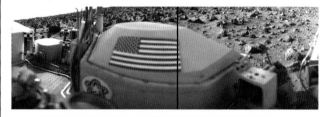

• See pages 22–23 for information on MARS.

RECENT PLANETERY PROBES

PROBE	LAUNCHED	DETAILS
Magellan	1989	Orbited Venus and produced detailed maps of its surface by radar
Galileo	1989	Surveyed Jupiter and its moons before plunging into Jupiter's atmosphere in 2003
Mars Pathfinder	1996	Landed the rover, *Sojourner*, on Mars in 1997
Cassini-Huygens	1997	Touring Saturn and its moons, landed the *Huygens* mini-probe on Saturn's moon, Titan, in 2005
Mars Exploration	2003	The rovers, *Spirit* and *Opportunity*, landed on Mars in 2004 and found evidence of water on Mars.

10 EARLY MOON PROBES

The Moon has been visited by a series of probes, some manned and some robotic.

In 1959, *Luna 2* became the first space probe to hit the Moon, while its successor took the first photographs of the far side. In 1966, *Luna 9* made the first controlled landing on the Moon, and in 1967, *Surveyor 3* (pictured right) dug a trench in the Moon's soil. *Luna 16* brought back a sample of Moon dust to Earth in 1970, while the same year its successor landed a rover vehicle, *Lunokhod 1*. Its probe was *Luna 17*.

SALYUT SPACE STATIONS		
STATION	LAUNCHED	RETURNED
Salyut 1	4/19/71	10/11/71
Salyut 2	4/4/73	5/28/73
Salyut 3	6/25/74	8/24/75
Salyut 4	12/26/74	2/3/77
Salyut 5	6/22/76	8/8/77
Salyut 6	9/29/77	7/29/82
Salyut 7	4/19/82	2/7/91

LIVING IN SPACE

People can stay in space for months or years at a time by living on orbiting space stations. Russia has launched eight space stations—seven *Salyut* stations and *Mir*. Meanwhile, the USA used rockets and spacecraft left over from the *Apollo* missions to create the *Skylab* space station. Now Russia, the USA, and more than a dozen other countries have come together to built the *International Space Station* (ISS). Space stations allow scientists to carry out long-term experiments and observations, and to study how people adapt to long periods in space.

SALYUT SPACE STATIONS

Salyut 1 was launched by the Soviet Union in 1971. It was the world's first space station.

- The *Salyut* space stations measured 42 feet long by up to 14 feet across.

- *Salyut 1–5* had one docking port, where a transfer spacecraft could attach.

- *Salyuts* 6 and 7 had two docking ports.

- A *Salyut* space station weighed about 21 tons.

- *Salyut* 6 and 7 could be refueled, which enabled them to stay in orbit for longer.

- *Salyut* 7 spent nearly nine years in orbit.

The 342-foot long *Salyut 7* on display in 1984 in Helsinki, Finland.

SKYLAB MISSIONS		
MISSION	LAUNCHED	LENGTH
Skylab 1	5/14/73	N/A
Skylab 2	5/25/73	28 days
Skylab 3	7/28/73	59 days
Skylab 4	11/16/73	84 days

Skylab astronaut Alan Bean.

SKYLAB SPACE STATION

Skylab was the United States' only space station.

- Launched on May 14, 1973 and spent more than six years in orbit. It was shaken so much during launch that one of its solar panels was torn off.

- *Skylab* was 118 feet long, with a spacecraft docked, and up to 21.5 feet wide.

- Three three-person *Skylab* crews took tens of thousands of photographs of the Earth and studied the Sun using *Skylab's* solar observatory.

- *Skylab* re-entered the Earth's atmosphere on July 11, 1979.

Skylab in orbit at the end of its mission.

MIR SPACE STATION

Space station *Mir* with the shuttle *Atlantis*.

In 1986, the Soviet Union launched the first 20 modules of a new space station, called *Mir*, which means *peace*.

- Five more modules were added until the mid-1990s (see below).

- *Mir* spent just over 15 years in orbit.

- US space shuttles were able to dock with *Mir*.

- Seven shuttle astronauts spent a total of 32 months on *Mir*.

- In 1997, an unmanned *Progress* supply craft crashed into *Mir*, damaging its hull and solar panels.

- The longest time spent in space at one time is 437 days, achieved by Russian cosmonaut Valeriy Polyakov on *Mir*, from January 8,1994 to March 22, 1995.

- Toward the end, *Mir* had many breakdowns and molds were growing on its equipment.

- *Mir* re-entered the Earth's atmosphere on March 23, 2001.

- Several large pieces of the 143-ton space station survived re-entry and splashed down in the South Pacific Ocean, east of New Zealand.

MIR MODULES

MODULE	LAUNCHED	USED FOR
Core module	1986	Command center and accommodation
Kvant-1	1987	Astronomical observatory
Kvant-2	1989	Airlock for spacewalks
Kristall	1990	Processing materials
Spektr	1995	Remote sensing
Piroda	1996	Remote sensing

THE INTERNATIONAL SPACE STATION

ISS - HISTORY

In 1998, the first two modules of the *International Space Station* were launched and joined together in orbit.

- The first parts were called the *Zarya* module. *Zarya* was launched by a Russian *Proton* rocket in November 1998.

- In December 1998, the space shuttle added the *Unity* module, called *Unity Node*.

- In July 2000, the *Zvezda* service module was added.

- The first crew, called *Expedition 1*, arrived in November 2000.

- The *Destiny* module was added in February 2001.

- Airlocks, docking ports for spacecraft, and connecting frames have also been added.

• See pages 50–51
SPACE SHUTTLE (USA)

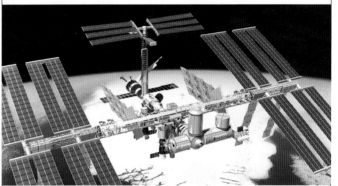

The International Space Station

ISS - FUTURE

- Its solar panels will have a span of 239.5 feet, almost the length of a soccer field.

- The living space inside will be bigger than in a jumbo jet.

- It will be about four times the size of *Mir* and five times the size of *Skylab*.

- It will have six laboratories, two habitation modules, and two logistics modules.

- The ISS orbits at a height of 248.5 miles above the surface of Earth.

- NASA is building a human-like robot, called *Robonaut*, to help ISS astronauts.

- Shuttle problems from 2003 have delayed the plannedcompletion of the main ISS units until at least 2010.

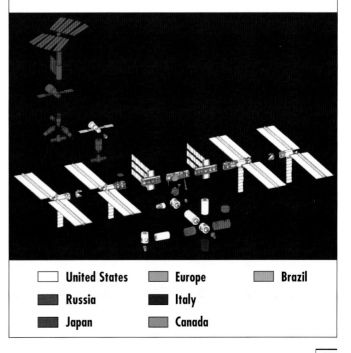

☐ **United States**	■ **Europe**	▨ **Brazil**
■ **Russia**	■ **Italy**	
■ **Japan**	▨ **Canada**	

GLOSSARY

Arachnoid A type of volcano with ridges around it that resembles a spider's body and legs when seen from above. First discovered and named on planet Venus.

Asteroid A lump of rock or metal, usually smaller than a planet and without an atmosphere or moons orbiting it, but also larger than a meteoroid. Most asteroids orbit the Sun. They are sometimes called *minor planets*.

Asteroid Belt The zone between the outermost inner planet Mars, and the innermost outer planet Jupiter, where millions of asteroids orbit the Sun.

Astronomy The study of planets, stars, moons, and other space bodies, also of space itself and the whole of the Universe. Astronomy is partly a practical science which involves observing and cataloging. see **Cosmology**

Astronomer Someone who studies the planets, stars, moons, and other bodies and objects in space.

Atmosphere The layer of gases surrounding a planet or star.

Axis An imaginary line passing through the middle of a star or planet, around which the object spins or rotates.

Big Bang An unimaginably gigantic explosion, thought to have happened at the beginning of the universe, more than 13 billion years ago, perhaps when space, time, and matter began.

Black hole A very small, dense, dark area of space with immensely powerful gravity, created when a star collapses to less than nothing and pulls in everything around it, including light.

Coma A bright glowing cloud, or "halo," around a body such as a comet.

Comet A relatively small ball of rock and ice, a "dirty snowball," orbiting the Sun on a very lop-sided path that may take it far beyond the distance of Pluto, to the Oort Cloud.

Constellation A pattern or picture seen in a group or cluster of stars as they are viewed from Earth.

Core The central part of a planet, moon, star, or other space object.

Corona The glowing ring or "halo" around the Sun, best seen during a solar eclipse when the Moon passes in front of the Sun.

Cosmology The development of astronomy dealing with the origin and evolution of the universe as a whole and how it works.

Crater A bowl- or dish-shaped hollow on a planet, moon, or asteroid, caused by another object crashing into it.

Crust The hard rocky outer layer of a planet, such as Earth.

Dark matter Invisible material that we cannot detect using scientific methods, but which is thought to make up a large percentage of the universe.

Day The amount of time it takes a planet or moon to spin round once on its axis, so that its nearest star returns to the same point in its sky.

Dwarf star A star that is smaller than the Sun.

Eclipse When one space object, such as a moon, goes between another object and a star, as when the Moon moves between the Sun and Earth, and casts a shadow on the Earth.

Equator An imaginary line around the middle of a planet or moon, at right angles to its axis of rotation (spin).

Galaxy A huge cluster of stars, planets and other objects, held together in space by gravity, and with immense distances of almost empty space to the next galaxies.

Gas giants Jupiter, Saturn, Uranus, and Neptune, the four largest outer planets in the solar system, which are made mostly of gases.

Giant star A star that is bigger than the Sun.

Gravity A force that makes any object or matter pull or attract other objects towards it. *Gravity* often refers to Earth's gravity, and *gravitational force* to the general name of the force that acts everywhere throughout the universe. The gravitational force is one of only four fundamental forces in the universe (the others are *electromagnetic force, strong nuclear force,* and *weak nuclear force*).

Hemisphere Half of a star, planet, moon, or similar object, usually either above (north) or below (south) of its equator.

Inner planets Mercury, Venus, Earth, and Mars, the four smaller and mainly rocky planets of the inner solar system, closest to the Sun.

Kuiper Belt A zone of orbiting asteroid- or comet-like objects in the outer solar system, orbiting the Sun beyond Neptune. Its existence was first proposed in 1951 by US astronomer Gerard Kuiper.

Lander A spacecraft, or part of one, designed to land on another space object, such as a planet or moon, or to plunge into the atmosphere of a gassy object, such as Jupiter. It can be crewed by astronauts, or unmanned and remote-controlled.

Lens A curved piece of glass that bends or refracts light, as used in telescopes, binoculars, and microscopes.

Lunar Having to do with Earth's moon.

Lunar eclipse When the Earth passes between the Sun and the Moon, casting a shadow on the Moon.

Mantle A layer of rock or other materials that lies between the core and the outer surface of a planet or moon.

Mass The amount of matter in an object. The numbers and types of atoms or their subatomic particles, independent of any gravity acting on them.

Meteor A meteoroid that enters Earth's atmosphere and burns up, appearing as a bright streak of light, also called a *shooting star* or *falling star*.

Meteorite A meteoroid that falls all the way to the Earth's surface.

Meteoroid A small chunk of rock, metal, ice, or a mixture of these, usually broken off a comet or asteroid.

Milky Way Our galaxy that contains the solar system.

Moon A space object that orbits a planet.

NASA (National Aeronautics and Space Administration) The government space agency of the USA.

Nebula A huge cloud of gas and dust in space, often where new stars are forming. A planetary nebula is a "shroud" of gas thrown off by an overheating or fading star.

Neutron star The small, incredibly dense remnant of a star that has exploded and collapsed into a ball of subatomic particles called *neutrons*.

Observatory A building or site where telescopes are used to observe objects in space.

Orbit To go around and around another object. The orbit of a planet or moon is its path around another object, such as the Sun. Most orbits are not circular, but elliptical (oval).

Orbiter A spacecraft or part of one that orbits its destination, rather than carrying out a fly-by or trying to land on the surface.

Oort Cloud A huge, ball-shaped cloud of comets and similar objects surrounding the whole solar system.

Planet A large, spherical, rocky and/or gassy object orbiting a star. Planets can be defined and

distinguished from other objects, such as asteroids, by their size, whether they orbit around a star, whether they have an atmosphere, and other features.

Pole The point on a rotating space object where the imaginary line around which it spins, the axis of rotation, passes through its surface.

Pulsar A rapidly rotating neutron star, that sends out beams of radio and other energy as it spins, like a lighthouse, and appears to flash or blink on and off.

Radar RAdio Direction And Ranging – a way of measuring shapes and distances of objects by bouncing or reflecting radio waves off them, and detecting and analyzing the reflections.

Satellite Any object that orbits another object in space, whether natural, such as a moon, or artificial, such as a space station. Often used for artificial or man-made objects orbiting Earth, such as communications satellites, comsats, and weather satellites, meteosats.

Sol The scientific name for the Sun.

Solar Having to do with the Sun.

Solar eclipse When the Moon passes between the Sun and the Earth, blocking out the Sun's light.

Solar System The Sun and all the planets, moons, and other objects that orbit around it or each other.

Spacecraft Any kind of vehicle or vessel built for travel in space. This name is often used for a crewed vehicle, one carrying astronauts.

Space probe A small, crewless spacecraft sent to explore space and send information or data back to Earth.

Space station A relatively large space base, for example, orbiting the Earth, where people can stay for long periods.

Star A relatively large space object that, for part of its existence, contains nuclear fusion reactions that produce heat and light, making it shine. There are many kinds of stars, such as white dwarfs, brown stars, and neutron stars.

Sunspot A darker, cooler area on the Sun's surface.

Supergiant star A very large, bright giant star.

Supernova The massive explosion at the end of a supergiant star's life.

Telescope A device that makes faraway things seem bigger, used for studying space. Optical telescopes detect light rays, while other kinds detect other forms of electromagnetic rays or radiation, such as radio waves, IR (infrared), UV (ultraviolet) and X-rays.

Transit When one relatively small space object is seen passing across the face of a larger, farther one, such as when Venus passes across the face of the Sun, as seen from Earth.

Trojans Two groups of asteroids following the same orbit around the Sun as Jupiter, one group in front of the planet and one behind.

Universe Everything that has ever existed, is existing, and could ever exist, including all of space and all its contents.

Year The amount of time a planet takes to complete one full orbit around its star.

INDEX